POWER

THE 50 TRUTHS

The Definitive Insider's Guide

DOUGLAS E. SCHOEN

Regan Arts.

I happily and lovingly dedicate this book to my mother, Carol Schoen, who has taught me more about life than anyone I have ever known.

"Most people can bear adversity. But if you wish to know what a man really is, give him power."

ROBERT G. INGERSOLL,
Abraham Lincoln: A Lecture (1895)

CONTENTS

PART FOUR
REWARD YOUR FRIENDS

INTRODUCTION

I AM WRITING to you about the world as it is, not the world as it ought to be. To my regret, and surely yours also, the two are not the same at all. In the world as it ought to be, people are honest, altruistic, and loyal. In the world as it is, they are too often, perhaps most often, none of these things. We discover, sometimes too late, they are deceptive, self-centered, and fickle. Yet this is the world we must each navigate. We have to manage the life that we have, so as best to achieve the life we ought to have. The people in power can afford to hire people like me to help them. The rest of us have to figure it out ourselves. Don't fret: I am here to help you.

You, too, can live like a leader, in your particular world. People may sometimes be greedy and narrow-minded, but they can also be brave and visionary and inspiring. In a lifetime as a political consultant, my clients have included a famous assassin–turned prime minister; a celebrated "terrorist" who also became the leader of his country; a bootlegger-pimp who was elected as a pioneering civil rights mayor; and a "Mafia priest" who rebuilt one of America's poorest slums. I have advised presidents and prime ministers and congresspeople and mayors and billionaire businessmen who raised up the poor, empowered the downtrodden, stood up for the persecuted, rose up against oppressors, battled rogue nuclear states, fought just wars, and made peace. Two of my clients—Yitzhak Rabin in Israel and Zoran Djindjic in Yugoslavia—were assassinated, as was the brother of a third, Medgar Evers in Mississippi. Three—Menachem Begin, Shimon Peres, and Rabin in Israel— won the Nobel Peace Prize. I advised President Bill Clinton how to handle the Monica Lewinsky scandal and conducted the first-ever presidential poll for Donald Trump. I helped both Ed Koch and Michael Bloomberg become mayor of New York. The lessons I have learned from them about the dynamics of power, you can learn too. These fifty principles of power, arranged in six simple steps, will help anyone, as they have helped me, optimize their prospects of success. My message: With a thought-out strategy, you, too, can do great things in your life.

"I was once hired by one of America's big lottery companies to conduct a poll to determine whether the public preferred a one-in-a-million chance of winning $1 million, or a one-in-five-hundred chance of winning $1,000."

As I would with a presidential candidate or a business titan, I offer you here a clear strategy. It is an unfortunate fact that many of us, if not most of us, suffer from poor decision-making. Time and again, we anticipate extraordinary outcomes that are so unlikely that we put our entire lives and livelihoods at risk. Dazzled by hope and desire, or by sheer need, we seem unable to weigh probabilities with proper perspective and rational judgment. We treat life as if it were a Lotto ticket. When we don't win, we are taken aback by outcomes that were perfectly foreseeable by others who were able to calculate correctly.

I was once hired by one of America's big lottery companies to conduct a poll to determine whether the public preferred a one-in-a-million chance of winning $1 million, or a one-in-five-hundred chance of winning $1,000. Trick question: I thought it was obvious that people would prefer the better odds. Not so. Some 70 percent of Americans prefer to take the long shot, despite the poorer chance of success.

The starting point of this book is the injunction not to do yourself self-harm. This is so fundamental that it should be self-evident, but it is surprisingly not. How many times do we see people who run a successful business try to expand too far or branch out into activities they are not suited for? This book reflects not only the lessons I have learned from those in power, but also the ways I have tried to manage my own life and my own business: with diligence, determination, and ambition, but also with circumspection.

You will find here a roadmap to accurately evaluate yourself and your circumstances and to play the cards you have at the right time to maximum effect. It will help you not just if you want to become Leader of the Free World; it will help you in your workplace, your community, your family, and even, for those unlucky enough to be there, your prison. We are all, after all, in our own prison. And we all seek to jailbreak in our own way. Some seek to escape to wealth and fame, others to political power, but most of us just seek our own independence. To help you free yourself, here in fifty simple truths is my insider's guide to power.

PART ONE

KNOW YOURSELF

The inscription on the Oracle at Delphi—

and surely the best advice anyone

ever gave anybody.

BILL CLINTON

President of the United States 1993-2001,
Governor of Arkansas 1979-1981, 1983-1992

White House intern Monica Lewinsky caught the eye of President Bill Clinton—but their relationship cost him his reputation.

Truth 1

FIRST, DO NO SELF-HARM

To this day, the medical profession lives by the Hippocratic Oath dating back to Ancient Greece. Its main injunction to doctors and nurses is to protect the patient: "First, do no harm." In the realm of power, the requirement is even more fundamental: "First, do no self-harm." Half the damage you will suffer, perhaps more, will be self-inflicted. Avoid it and you are already halfway there.

WITH MY HELP behind the scenes, Bill Clinton emerged triumphant from the 1996 election. Having successfully repositioned himself as a centrist after a brief *entente* with the Left, Clinton won re-election by almost 9 percentage points—the first Democratic president to win two full terms since Franklin Delano Roosevelt in 1936.

This spectacular victory set him up to be a potentially transformational president in an era of American world dominance after victory in the Cold War. Having boldly proclaimed that "the era of Big Government is over," he stood at the threshold of a major renovation of America that included finally grasping the nettle of Social Security reform. The post–Cold War economy was thriving and the stock market booming. Ultimately, however, a petty sexual scandal vitiated his precious second term and irreparably weakened his presidency.

These days, especially with the advent of the Me-Too movement, Bill Clinton has lost his broad popularity. Sometimes, Clinton can no longer even appear in public without sparking angry protests.

This is profoundly sad to me because his enormous contributions to politics and policy often go unremarked and unacknowledged. Having heard him speak a number of times privately, I feel it is a profound loss to America that Bill Clinton no longer has the public voice that he used to.

I watched this unraveling happen close up, in painful slow motion, from inside the White House.

Clinton is the most accomplished political operative I have ever met. A charismatic, working-class, southern white boy (and musician), he is the Elvis Presley of American politics: an absolute natural. He had it all: He could play a local crowd, he could analyze a state, he could think through a political problem, and he had more sincere compassion for people than virtually any other politician I have ever seen.

He asked me to join him midway through his first term as president to help him fight the 1996 election. For a political consultant, he was a dream. He operated by the Socratic method: asking questions. His view was that he would achieve a better result through a vigorous debate among advisers. I remember him instructing me, even beseeching me, "I don't want to hear what you think I want to hear. I want to hear what you think, fully and completely, always."

He is also one of the most attractive men I have met. When he would feast his eyes on a woman, and look into her eyes, he was mesmerizing. However, he was unable to control his urges despite the obvious self-harm it caused. Some women, like Juanita Broaddrick, Paula Jones, and Kathleen Willey, made accusations against him that literally boggled my mind.

Less than a year into his second term, I found myself mired in the scandal over the president's relationship with the twenty-two-year-old White House intern, Monica Lewinsky.

"I watched this unraveling happen close up, in painful slow motion, from inside the White House."

That the scandal blew up should really have been no surprise to me, and particularly to him, since Bill had already had a similar scare on the campaign trail in 1992 with a lounge-singer named Gennifer Flowers. But his wife, Hillary, stood by her man on 60 *Minutes* and Bill survived to fight another day.

Bill's encounters with Monica in the private hallway off the Oval Office proved a far greater threat than Flowers. She was not only much younger but was also his subordinate in the White House hierarchy. Bill insisted on TV, "I did not have sexual relations with that woman, Miss Lewinsky." His calculation was that he needed his support in the House of Representatives and only a categorical denial would do. I watched the White House surreptitiously mount a whispering campaign to discredit Lewinsky.

Although the Lewinsky scandal led to him becoming only the second president ever impeached by the House, Clinton, frankly, never understood the fundamental problem. He always insisted that the passive receipt of oral pleasure was not sex—a concept that someone who is not a former law professor like him might struggle to comprehend. Just as some men need a stiff drink in times of stress, he felt he needed sexual relief.

The "opportunity cost" of the scandal was immense—both for Clinton and America. Clinton was never able to reimagine government for a new era, as he had promised to do. There was also, I believe, a serious impact on national security. On August 20, 1998, Clinton ordered cruise missile strikes against al-Qaeda in Sudan and Afghanistan in retaliation for the bombing of the US embassies in Kenya and Tanzania. The strikes, named Operation Infinite Reach, missed Osama bin Laden. Beset by the Lewinsky affair, the Clinton Administration lost focus and leverage to pursue him aggressively and bin Laden struck again on 9/11.

Clinton's considered explanation of his misbehavior with Monica was essentially "just because I could"—a comment that displays a remarkable lack of self-knowledge for a man of such obvious intelligence. In his memoir, *My Life*, he called it "selfish stupidity." To this day, he appears befuddled by the Monica fuss. When she co-produced a TV miniseries about the saga in 2021, the fact that he was unable to offer her the apology she is owed left me disappointed and saddened.

It is a blindness that has damaged not just Bill Clinton himself but also his wife, politically as well as emotionally. When Hillary ran against Donald Trump for the presidency in 2016, Trump fended off pressure over his "Grab 'em by the p—y" comments by invoking Bill's sexual misdeeds. Longtime Republican operative Roger Stone co-wrote a 2016 book titled *The Clintons' War on Women* and invited Bill's accusers Broaddrick, Willey, and Jones to embarrass Hillary at the second presidential debate in St Louis. This was a deliberate act of diversion that may well have distracted Hillary Clinton. It further damaged her chances of becoming America's first female president. What Bill considered innocent dalliances ended up hurting not just himself but also Hillary. Harming your wife also counts as self-harm.

DONALD TRUMP

President of the United States 2017–2021

The idea that the owner of soon-to-be bankrupt casinos could be elected president seemed ridiculous when I did Donald Trump's first presidential poll in 1987.

Truth 2

YOUR WEAKNESSES ARE YOUR STRENGTHS...

People generally underrate their weaknesses. But it is important to recognize them—and not just to avoid them—because a weakness is often a strength in another context.

I DID THE FIRST POLL for Donald Trump to test his chances of being elected president of the United States—in 1987! At the time, I thought the whole thing was ridiculous. The guy was flirting with bankruptcy with his casinos in Atlantic City; he did not listen to anybody; he could be abusive; and he did not pay his bills.

My first meeting with him took place in his office on the now-famous twenty-sixth floor of Trump Tower. He was much more low-key than he appears now, and much more uncertain about how to present himself, but equally quick to act like he knew better than you.

In contrast to what you read in the media, Trump in person is actually a very smart and thoughtful man—if he is not under the gun. Trump, however, feels under the gun any time he is in a meeting with more than two people. On such occasions—and particularly if there was a woman present—he feels an absolute need to dominate the conversation. Which he does.

I worked closely with him doing market research on his casinos and his short-lived airline, the Trump Shuttle, so I can confirm one of his best-known flaws: You could not do a standard presentation to him. I remember showing up with fifty to a hundred slides to do a presentation to him, and getting through just three or four slides before he started to dominate the conversation. His inability to listen is now legendary. It is the narrative of just about every book and article written about his administration.

"He didn't even ask what I was doing there unannounced. 'Donald, you've got to pay,' I declared."

Trump's niece Mary, who has a PhD in clinical psychology, insists her uncle's domineering behavior and reality-defying hyperbole are the consequence of his upbringing by his "sociopathic" father, Fred, the second-generation German immigrant who built the family's real-estate empire in the New York borough of Queens. In Mary Trump's telling, Donald was forced to become his own cheerleader to impress his father. "By the time of his election, Donald met any challenges to his sense of superiority with anger, his fear and vulnerabilities so effectively buried that he didn't even have to acknowledge they existed," she wrote.

Mary, the daughter of Donald Trump's older brother, Freddy, comes, of course, from a line of the family that was virtually disinherited because Freddy, an alcoholic, died when he was just forty-two. The family drama she describes in her book *Too Much and Never Enough: How my Family Created the World's Most Dangerous Man* is often heart-rending. After she complains to her grandmother Mary—after whom she is named—that she has been cut out of the family inheritance, her grandmother writes Mary out of her own will as well. But what is a problem around the Thanksgiving table is not necessarily a problem in power politics.

In politics you have to have thick skin. You have to be willing to deal with the slings and arrows from your opponents, and do what Donald Trump did singularly well, which is to stand up to criticism. He is able to do that in a way that actually brings in more votes rather than costs him support. What to Mary Trump is hard-heartedness can in politics be called resilience.

Donald's first tentative foray into national politics came on September 2, 1987, when he placed a full-page open letter "To the American People" in the *New York Times*, the *Washington Post*, and the *Boston Globe*. The ad complained that America's allies were freeloading by failing to pay their fair share for the United States defending them, which later became a familiar Trump theme. The man famed for his fragile ego concluded with a very Trumpian punch line: "Let's not let our great country be laughed at any more."

Our 1987 poll concluded, as I had always expected, that Trump was very unlikely to be elected president the following year. In a poll, you game-test the campaign to answer a simple question that is not answered simply: How easy or difficult is it to elect the candidate? We asked people whether they had heard of Donald Trump and whether they would vote for him. We then offered voters tidbits of information about the would-be candidate to determine whether that information made them more or less likely to support him. Though he was already a tabloid figure in New York City, we found that he still had little name recognition nationwide. This was before he hosted *The Apprentice* on TV for fourteen seasons. While we found there was resonance for a man with his message, he had just 15 to 20 percent favorability. There was not yet the current scale of anti-systemic anger that would favor an outsider candidate. The main obstacle, however, proved to be the state of his Atlantic City casinos, which were heading inexorably into insolvency. The idea of running for president while you had a bankrupt casino was, to say the least, very problematic.

Typically, as we now know, Trump did not pay me for the poll. The outstanding amount was the then not-inconsiderable sum of $80,000. So I decided to take matters into my own hands. One Friday, I had lunch with a friend at the Harvard Club—a place that is culturally about as far from Donald Trump as it is possible to be, but geographically lies just thirteen blocks from Trump Tower. As I was walking home up Fifth Avenue, I decided to go into Trump Tower and confront him. In those pre-9/11 days, there was little security. I just took the elevator to the twenty-sixth floor, brushed past the receptionist, and strode into his office, where he was sitting. He looked up, showing no surprise. He didn't even ask what I was doing there unannounced. "Donald, you've got to pay," I declared. He looked at me and gestured at a stack of papers standing about eighteen inches high on his desk. "You see this pile?" he asked. "I've got all these invoices to pay. You want me to pull yours out?" I responded with what I thought was a quick and clever reply. "But, Donald, I only need one check." Without fuss, he said, "That's okay." He wrote out a check and handed it to me, and I went straight out to the bank.

His reaction has always impressed me. I think he thought my unexpected appearance and demand showed the kind of person I was—and he appreciated my chutzpah. Rather than be offended, I think he thought I'd shown a little moxie. The encounter did not generate any ill-will at all.

If he were a buffoon and an idiot, as so often portrayed in the media, he couldn't have pulled off winning the presidency. He beat ten other candidates in the Republican primary and then defeated the Clinton machine. Even though Hillary Clinton was unpopular, she still had a war chest of $1.8 billion that dwarfed Trump's less-than-$1 billion.

In 1987, I did not think he'd be president. But when I saw his staying power, his resilience, and his ability to manipulate public opinion, I was not surprised. Whether it is an adaptation to a dysfunctional father, or whether it's tenacity that goes off the charts, we have never had anyone in American life do what Trump did. It was an extraordinary accomplishment for a man who had never been in politics. The last outsider to win the presidency was Dwight D. Eisenhower—a five-star general who won World War II.

Throughout his term in office, Trump doubled down on the traits that had got him so far: overweening self-confidence, domineering behavior, his stubborn refusal to listen to anybody other than himself. While they had served as a source of strength to him in winning power, they proved a weakness once he was in power. If he had not acted as crazy as he did about the COVID-19 virus, if he had just spoken to all of us about the need to pull together, if he had just acknowledged that there were no answers and that he was trying to balance public health with the economic well-being of the country, which we all knew anyway, and if he had been willing just to wear a mask, he'd have been re-elected in 2020. I don't think there is any doubt of that.

EHUD BARAK

Prime Minister of Israel 1999–2001

Ehud Barak, left, disguised himself as an aircraft technician to rescue hostages in the 1972 hijacking at Tel Aviv's Lod Airport.

Truth 3

...AND YOUR STRENGTHS ARE YOUR WEAKNESSES

We are often told to "play to our strengths." But there is a peril to this also. Personality is seamless so that even the most obvious strengths are rarely just strengths. They can also be unappreciated weaknesses.

IT IS NOT EVERY DAY that I meet a highly trained assassin. By the time of our first encounter, Ehud Barak was Israel's most decorated soldier. He was famous above all for cross-dressing as a woman for a daredevil commando raid into Lebanon to assassinate three Palestinian Liberation Organization figures. In 1973, Barak, then commander of Israel's special forces, Sayeret Matkal, had disembarked at night from a boat on the Beirut waterfront and led the assault on three apartments on the city's Rue Verdun. The successful attack became the stuff of legend, later featured in the 2005 Steven Spielberg movie *Munich*. Barak and two other members of the thirteen-man squad disguised themselves in drag with wigs and flared pants as female partygoers with their boyfriends. Barak, then thirty-one, played the "mother" of the group, carrying the team's radio in a large purse. When his real wife woke up to find him back at home after the successful completion of the mission, he was still wearing his blue eye shadow and mascara.

"I could tell that he was a trained killer: He had a steely coldness in his eyes."

It was a very unlikely preparation for our first experience of working together: a business meeting in Florida to discuss marketing strategy for SlimFast diet products. Barak, who had recently completed his term as Israeli chief of staff, was serving as an adviser to S. Daniel "Danny" Abraham, the owner of SlimFast and the founder of a think tank on Middle East peace. Barak and I flew down to West Palm Beach on Abraham's private plane to offer our insights. He was by then somewhat portly. Obviously, he had never used SlimFast. Even though we were discussing diet products mostly used by downscale women, it was immediately clear to me that he had a brilliant strategic mind. I could tell, however, that he was a trained killer: He had a steely coldness in his eyes.

A small number of people you meet in life are very smart, and an even smaller number are ruthlessly brilliant, but most are neither. Barak was both very, very smart and ruthlessly brilliant. My later dealings with him, as a political consultant, confirmed that view—but also allowed me to see how self-confident brilliance was also his Achilles' heel.

After a thirty-six-year military career in which he had commanded Israel's special forces, led a tank battalion across the Suez Canal in the 1973 Yom Kippur War, run military intelligence, and finally become chief of staff, Barak decided to enter the battlefield of Israeli politics. Prime Minister Yitzhak Rabin, one of Israel's long line of soldier-statesmen, also a previous chief of staff, asked Barak to become interior minister. But Rabin was gunned down at a peace rally by a Jewish extremist in 1995 in an attack that shocked Israel. His successor, Shimon Peres, appointed Barak as foreign minister. When Peres lost the election the following year to his right-wing challenger, Benjamin "Bibi" Netanyahu, Barak called me in to sound out his own prospects.

At the end of 1997, I was hired with my colleague Zev Furst to provide Barak with a comprehensive polling picture of the electorate. Bibi Netanyahu had served under Barak in the Sayeret Matkal, as had his older brother, Yoni Netanyahu. Bibi and Barak had worked closely in the special forces. In 1972, Barak had picked the more junior Bibi as one of his team to storm a hijacked Sabena airliner that had landed at Tel Aviv's Lod Airport. Yoni, the more senior and battle-tested of the two brothers, had been training in the Negev desert and arrived later at the scene demanding to be added to one of the assault teams. Following an unwritten Sayeret Matkal rule, Barak refused to allow the two brothers to go into harm's way together. The brothers discussed it among themselves and left it up to Barak to make the choice. Barak chose Bibi, telling Yoni: "Today it's Bibi." Dressed in white overalls as mechanics, Barak's force seized the Boeing 707, killing two of the hijackers and capturing the other two. One of the ninety passengers was also shot dead. Bibi's arm was grazed by a bullet in the fight.

Yoni, who became Barak's deputy, infiltrated into Beirut with him for the Rue Verdun raid (though Yoni was not required to dress as a woman). Then in 1976, Sayeret Matkal was scrambled to deal with another hijacked airliner, this time at Uganda's Entebbe airport. By then, Yoni had succeeded Barak as the chief of special forces—and was also his downstairs neighbor in their apartment building in Ramat HaSharon, north of Tel Aviv. Barak was named the overall commander of the Entebbe rescue operation with Yoni charged with leading the audacious assault. It was in this battle, which successfully freed 102 of the 106 hostages, that Yoni was shot dead. Barak asked his wife to go downstairs to break the news of his death to Yoni's wife.

Despite this intense history, Barak gave me no sign that he had more than a passing acquaintance with Bibi Netanyahu. Even as the 1999 election drew closer, we had no discussion at all about what kind of man his opponent, Bibi, was. His sole focus was: "What is the best way to win this election? Tell me what to do and I will do it." Barak spoke of himself as a general seeking "intelligence," not a politician seeking strategic advice.

Barak publicly announced he was hiring our rival pollster Stanley Greenberg along with Democratic Party strategists James Carville and Bob Shrum. Greenberg had played a key role in the victories of both Bill Clinton and Britain's Tony Blair. Nevertheless, I continued to provide separate polling advice to Barak in the background.

Barak told me he hired Greenberg, Carville, and Shrum for their public-relations impact and insisted that my Israeli colleague Zev Furst and I provided him with better intelligence. A general, he explained, needed multiple levels of information. Our role in the campaign was run like a covert military operation. The funding was opaque. We were paid through an organization called the Israel Policy Forum, run by Jonathan D. Jacoby, who formally commissioned our polling. It became clear to me that Isaac "Bougie" Herzog, the son of a former Israeli president and now president of Israel himself, had some informal oversight over our work—though precisely what, I was never sure. Furst and I briefed Barak face-to-face. In any event, no charges were ever brought or apparently contemplated.

Barak's view was that he was smarter than everybody about everything. Which was, to a very large degree, true. But he also made it very clear there was no warmth or feeling, We were there to effectuate a result that he believed we were uniquely situated to provide. And that was that. I came out of that campaign with no feelings about him: no empathy and no sense of loyalty. I was basically a surreptitious hired gun to provide sub-rosa information to the commander.

Based on our polling results, we recommended that he embrace a single election message: "Israel doesn't trust Bibi. Bibi has failed." The election strategy worked perfectly. Barak won the 1999 election by a landslide 58.5 percent to Bibi's 41.5 percent. But within two years, after a failed attempt at

Camp David peacemaking with the Palestinians, and pulling Israeli forces out of southern Lebanon, he was turned out of office as one of the most unpopular Israeli prime ministers ever.

His great strength was that he was ruthlessly focused on getting things done, using information to achieve a result. People, though, were interchangeable to him. Everything was a battle; nothing was about building a relationship; nothing was about building friendships or professional relationships. It was all a tactical battle to achieve outcomes, which in the short term worked very well but in the long term worked much less well.

Barak, whose military training taught him to always study any failures, offers an intriguing self-criticism in his autobiography, *My Country, My Life*. He attributes his emotional aloofness to the sacrifice, physical labor, and life-and-death struggles of his generation of Israelis who created the state from the desert. But he does not entirely bat away the diagnosis made by some political rivals and pundits in his career that he had a "touch of Asperger's," a term once used to describe people on the autism spectrum who displayed a lack of empathy for others but also greater focus and talent for abstract ideas, music, and mathematics. Indeed, Barak, who plays Beethoven to relax and studied theoretical physics at university, even made an apology for his strength-cum-weakness in a public letter when he sought the leadership of the Labor Party for a second time in 2007: "I realize now there are no shortcuts and leadership is not a one-man show."

He was a magnificent general, but you cannot act like a general in democratic politics.

CARTER BURDEN

New York City Councilman 1970–1977

Carter Burden campaigning for New York City Council in 1969 from the back of an old Paris bus provided by the expensive French restaurant Lutèce.

Truth 4

YOU ARE NOT ENTITLED

You might be lucky or you might be unlucky in the circumstances of your birth. Probably, like most people, you are both. But one thing is certain: You must not approach life assuming you can ride your privilege to success. Whatever advantages you may have inherited, you must not assume you are entitled to success.

THIS IS THE CAUTIONARY TALE of the rich, aristocratic, and glamorous US president who never was.

When I was a bright young politico, Shirley Carter Burden Jr. was wildly promoted by the press as a future occupant of the White House. On November 7, 1971, the *New York Times* opined: "Like Kent cigarettes, Carter Burden has got it all together, and one can't help but observe that—in an age of politics by electronics, when the race is just about always to the wealthiest and most telegenic candidate—he has virtually every qualification necessary to end up ultimately in residence at 1600 Pennsylvania Avenue."

As the great-great-grandson of Cornelius "The Commodore" Vanderbilt, Burden was an heir to the family's fabulous "Gilded Age" shipping and railway fortune—and a cousin of CNN anchorman Anderson Cooper. He was born in Beverly Hills, where his father had run off to marry the actress-niece of the swashbuckling silent-movie star Douglas Fairbanks Sr. Burden grew up a Hollywood child. His first girlfriend was Charlie Chaplin's daughter Geraldine. After Harvard and Columbia Law School, Burden went to work for Senator Robert F. Kennedy, to whom he would often be—unjustly to Bobby Kennedy—compared.

Carter landed in New York with a young wife who came from an equally star-studded lineage. Still a prominent New York figure to this day, Amanda Burden, nicknamed "Ba" for "baby," is a descendant of the first chief justice of the US Supreme Court, John Jay. Her father was an heir to the Standard Oil fortune. When she was a little girl, her mother, "Babe," had remarried William Paley, the powerhouse who ran CBS television and radio.

"The couple quickly became not just coveted New York socialites but leading 'socialitists,' as 'socialist socialites' were dubbed at the time."

At one of their early dates, Carter announced to Amanda that he wanted to be president. "I think I can do the job," he told her immodestly. Ensconced in the exclusive River House cooperative at the eastern end of Manhattan's Fifty-Second Street, the couple quickly became not just coveted New York socialites but leading "socialitists," as "socialist socialites" were dubbed at the time. Tom Wolfe, in an era-defining *New York* magazine article, cited them as prime examples of "Radical Chic." The couple threw the first Manhattan party for California farmworkers' leader Cesar Chavez. Like others of their clan, the Burdens hired white servants. *Vogue* magazine reported that "Mrs. Burden, with the help of a maid, is learning how to keep house." Shirley Carter Burden Jr. dropped the "Shirley" and the "Jr." to become a man of the people. The *New York Times* archly suggested he dropped his first name lest people confuse him with the first-ever Black congresswoman, Shirley Chisholm. "Carter Burden . . ." Wolfe concluded, "developed what can only be termed the first Total Radical Chic lifestyle."

Still just twenty-eight, Carter began what was meant to be a procession to the White House by running for the New York City Council in 1969. His idea of pounding the pavement was to tour the slums in an old Paris bus lent to him by the fashionable French restaurant Lutèce. The district in East Harlem actually lay beneath the elevated railway tracks his family had once owned. Propelled by his celebrity, and the endorsement of the *New York Times*, Carter won with 81 percent of the vote. *New York* magazine, epicenter of the colorful and opinionated New Journalism, ran a cover of him and Amanda alongside photos of the ultimate glamor power couple: John F. Kennedy and Jackie Kennedy.

The next step for Carter was to conquer the New York Democratic Party machine. That was where I came in.

The contest was to decide the next Democratic "boss" of Manhattan, the leader of the New York County Democrats. Carter, a self-styled Reform Democrat, wanted to take down the existing boss, Frank Rossetti. Assemblyman Rossetti symbolized the old corrupt Tammany Hall bribery and patronage system that had run New York City politics for decades. He had risen to the position after serving as chauffeur to the previous boss, Carmine DeSapio. If Carter, a self-styled Reform Democrat, could break the Tammany Hall grip on New York, he would be the new king of city politics—and on his way toward the White House. The stakes were that high.

Carter's idea was to run a Reform Democrat as a primary challenger against Rossetti in his East Harlem stronghold. The chosen candidate was a young lawyer named Eugene Nardelli. My job, at age eighteen, was to get him elected.

I had been introduced to Burden by our common friend Antonio "Tony" Olivieri, who had helped me get into Harvard and had gone to Columbia Law School with Burden. To give him his due, Tony had warned me. "You should meet Carter," he told me. "But please understand: He's a specialist in getting other people to live his life for him." Tony said he had written all Burden's papers to get him through law school.

Our first strategy meeting was held over breakfast at the Burdens' duplex at the River House. Notwithstanding the early hour, Burden wore a smoking jacket like a potentate and, in his latest affectation, was puffing on a pipe. He was not quite thirty years old, yet was already living his own version of what he thought rich people were supposed to do—all, of course, with inherited money. Also present were Nardelli in one of his flashy suits; his running mate, Elba Diaz, a court translator; and her campaign-manager husband, Angelo Guerrero, a laborer. Both Diaz and her husband were scruffy and morbidly obese. "Ba" also appeared, as slim and elegant as ever, making it perfectly obvious why she had become a permanent fixture on New York's Best Dressed List.

Breakfast was served by those same politically correct white waiters, themselves contenders for the Best Dressed List in natty white jackets and gloves. Guerrero asked for an egg. A disdainful waiter asked him if he meant a two-minute egg, a two-and-a-half-minute egg, or a three-minute egg. Exasperated, Guerrero exploded: "I want an egg!"

Burden took a desultory interest in the discussions. Even at my tender age, it was immediately obvious to me that the man was a dilettante.

All those vaunted White House ambitions were just smoke and mirrors, fueled by money, celebrity, and the New Journalism. After Bobby Kennedy's assassination, he had bathed in the reflected glory—even though he had been little more than a glorified intern in the senator's office. After my breakfast meeting in the River House, I came away with a stark conclusion: *This dog don't hunt.*

Despite the high stakes, Burden spent most of the primary campaign at his mansion in the Hamptons rather than showing up for Nardelli in East Harlem, even though it overlapped with his own Council district. Perhaps needless to say, Nardelli lost. The Tammany guys stayed in control. I remember saying to myself at the time, "This is not how you lead your life, this is not how you operate, this is not how you take on the establishment, this is not how you produce change, this is not how you effectuate successful outcomes."

The postscript to the story is both sad and hopeful. Carter and Amanda broke up the following year in a divorce that the *New York Times* predicted "future social critics may use to mark the end of the 60's." Carter failed in a 1978 run for Congress and never went any higher in politics than New York City Hall—certainly nowhere near the White House. He used his inherited money to purchase *New York* magazine, where Wolfe had so mocked him. But he remained a lonely and bored man, who would leaf through shopping catalogs for hours buying things, and died at age fifty-four.

Amanda "Ba" Burden, by contrast, has worked tirelessly to shed her socialite image. Her whole life since has been a rebuke to the glossy magazine reports that she had dropped out of Wellesley College just so she could prepare for her wedding to Carter. With quiet grace and a scrupulous attention to detail, she went back to college and eventually obtained a master's degree in urban planning specializing in the unglamorous topic of solid-waste management. She would eventually chair the City Planning Commission. Though she was never considered a figure of substance in politics or government, she in fact became one of the singular forces of urban planning and development in the twenty-first century. Entitled by birth as she may have been, she put in the hard work and achieved what her ex-husband conspicuously failed to.

SHIMON PERES

President of Israel 2007–2014,
Prime Minister of Israel 1995–1996, 1984–1986

Shimon Peres always dreamed of peace for Israel. On September 13, 1993, as foreign minister, he was the official Israeli signatory on the Oslo Peace Accords at the White House.

Truth 5

FOLLOW
YOUR MUSE

No one ever succeeded at anything without a passion for what they do. It is the single most important marker of success. The starting point is to identify what excites you. Then just follow your muse, wherever it may lead you.

SHIMON PERES WAS BORN in a *shtetl* in the forest in what is now Belarus in 1923, the son of a timber merchant and a librarian — and a distant relative of the future American actress Lauren Bacall. The village of three streets of rudimentary wooden houses had no electricity or running water. As a boy, he would hitch a carriage ride to the nearest train station three miles away to watch the farewell parties for the Jewish pioneers departing to pursue their people's multi-millennial dream of a return from exile to the Promised Land. It was inconceivable to the precocious young child that one day he would himself become president of the then-nonexistent state of Israel.

I worked both for and against Peres as a political consultant in Israel. In person, he was a brilliant, charming, and gracious man. Though seen as a political schemer, to me he seemed disconnected from the ins and outs of the struggle for power. He was a visionary who was as committed to ideas as he was to power. He could see far into the future, but could not see into next week. Many called him romantic and naive, but it was his vision that carried him onward. "I prefer to be an idealist than to be cynical," Peres once explained to Canada's *Globe and Mail* newspaper. "Pessimists and optimists die the same way, they just live differently."

Till his death in 2016 at age ninety-three, Peres always argued for the role of imagination in politics. His autobiography was titled, *No Room for Small Dreams*. Better to chase big dreams and suffer the consequences than to limit your ambitions just to get by, he argued. He taught his children: "Count the number of dreams you have and compare them with the number of achievements you've had. If you have more dreams than achievements, then you are still young."

"As a boy, he would hitch a carriage ride to the nearest train station three miles away to watch the farewell parties for the Jewish pioneers departing to pursue their people's multi-millennial dream of a return from exile to the Promised Land."

His own father left from that train station outside the shtetl to pursue his own Zionist dream when Peres was just nine. Peres and the rest of the family joined him in the then-British Mandate of Palestine two years later. In his late teens, as Jews settled back in their ancestral land, Peres helped found a *kibbutz* farming community in northern Israel. Assigned to be a shepherd, he sat with his flock beneath the stars and dreamed of becoming a poet or an architect, to build something either from words or from stones. He ended up writing eleven books—and helped to build a whole new state.

Millions of Jews were being exterminated in Europe in Nazi death camps. Peres's own beloved grandfather, the rabbi of their shtetl, was locked by German troops into his synagogue with the other Jews of the village. The Nazi soldiers set fire to the wooden building and burned them all alive. With the *Shoah*, the age-old Jewish project of a return to Zion took on extreme urgency to save the Jewish people.

Despite his later reputation as Israel's preeminent dove and advocate of a land-for-peace deal, Peres played a decisive role in arming Jews to protect their new state, both before and after its creation. His mentor, Zionist leader David Ben-Gurion, summoned him from the kibbutz to help the Haganah, the underground Jewish army in British Palestine. Ben-Gurion handed him a scruffy shopping list of weapons the Haganah needed to ward off the expected invasion by Arab nations when Israel declared independence. The list had two columns: one for the supplies the Haganah had already obtained and one for those it still needed. The supplies already in hand included "six million bullets." Peres thought that sounded like a lot, but Ben-Gurion explained the Jewish force would need one million bullets a day in the war. The chief of staff had just quit because he was not willing to wage war with less than a week's worth of ammunition.

Peres, with zero expertise but overwhelming dedication to the cause, went on secret missions with fake passports to stockpile the guns he needed, mostly from Czechoslovakia. Israel fended off the Arab attack and the Haganah became the Israeli Defense Forces. Peres was named secretary of the new state's Navy, even though he admitted: "My experience consisted of moderate proficiency at breaststroke and one childhood attempt to launch a raft off the coast of Tel Aviv." Ben-Gurion, who became Israel's first prime minister, sent him to Washington as a military attaché even though he spoke little English, and then named him director of the entire defense ministry. In that role he secretly negotiated with France to build a nuclear reactor at Dimona, which gave Israel its all-important nuclear deterrent.

With Israel's defense secured, Peres pivoted to peacemaking. Once a proponent of Jewish settlements from the Sinai Desert to the Jordanian border, he metamorphosed into the leading advocate of "land-for-peace." Once known in Israel as "Mr. Security," he became "Mr. Peace." As foreign minister, he was the driving force and official Israeli signatory of the 1993 Oslo Peace Accords that granted limited Palestinian self-government. It won him a Nobel Peace Prize.

"When I thought that Israel was in danger, I was a terrible hawk," he explained. "I thought it my duty to do whatever I could to defend Israel to make it stronger. But that wasn't a purpose; this was a must. Once I felt that we could go for peace, I changed, because that is a purpose. War is a must; peace is a goal."

Although he served as prime minister for two brief spells, plus another in an acting capacity, Peres was always accounted an unsuccessful politician. At the age of eighty-three, however, he was elected by the Knesset as the ninth president of Israel, the state he had helped create. "Permit me to remain an optimist," he insisted in his inaugural address." Permit me to be a dreamer of his people." From his childhood in the shtetl, Israel had been his muse.

MICHAEL BLOOMBERG

Mayor of New York City 2002–2013

Michael Bloomberg told me the biggest surprise he found in politics was how little most politicians care about the broader public interest. Here the then-mayor of New York City is pursuing his passion for education at P.S. 282 in Brooklyn on March 20, 2006.

Truth 6

PURSUE A PURPOSE GREATER THAN YOURSELF

You must never lose sight of the purposes of power. Self-glorification is not enough. You have greater strength and appeal if you are acting for others as well as for yourself.

WHEN I WAS FIRST INVITED to meet Michael Bloomberg for lunch at the Paper Moon restaurant on New York's East Fifty-Eighth Street in 1998, I flattered myself that he wanted to know what my polling company could do for his growing financial media business, Bloomberg LP.

The son of a bookkeeper in the Boston suburbs, he had built his own company from scratch with the near-miraculous Bloomberg Terminal that offered Wall Streeters instant access to a vast array of market data. Then fifty-four, Bloomberg had already made his first billion dollars—and was well on his way to his seventieth. Yes, that is $70 billion with a "b."

To my dismay, Bloomberg seemed pleasantly uninterested in my business pitch. Only when he began asking me questions about the New York political scene did he come alive. By the time I had finished my *tortellini alla crema*, I realized he was interested in something quite different: He wanted to go into politics himself.

Bloomberg later told then-Mayor Rudolph Giuliani that he was interested in four jobs in politics: US president, United Nations secretary-general, World Bank president, and mayor of New York. He had zero chance of becoming the UN chief and little of getting elected president straightaway. He would make an exceptional head of the World Bank, traditionally a US appointment. But it was very clear to me at that lunch that he had set his sights on becoming mayor.

> ## "By the time I had finished my *tortellini alla crema*, I realized he was interested in something quite different: He wanted to go into politics himself."

As we walked back to Bloomberg's office after lunch, I felt compelled to warn him of the perils of big-time politics. He was inviting a level of media scrutiny that he could find very uncomfortable. He brushed off my concern, saying that had never put him off before. He was motivated, he said, by concern about the worsening racial and social divide in the city and wanted to bring people together. Within a year, I was working on his fledgling campaign. His instinct was right: One of our first polls found that, although New Yorkers credited the loudmouthed incumbent with slashing crime, they wanted a "Giuliani without the divisiveness."

By that point, Bloomberg had achieved such success in life that he was asking himself: "Is this it?" For most people, that would indeed have been it. He already had more money than he could ever spend and was making huge donations to worthy causes. But he wanted to contribute more. He had a vision of how to make America better and backed himself to implement it. Despite his large charitable gifts, he had run up against the limits of philanthropy. There are some things you cannot get done simply by donating money. You need political power. Bloomberg wanted to use his skillset, his leadership qualities and management prowess, to effect meaningful change beyond what he could achieve with philanthropy. He wanted, in short, to use his talents to be useful in the world. I remember him saying to me: "I do not want to be known or remembered simply as a guy who wrote big checks."

As he records in his autobiography, *Bloomberg on Bloomberg*, his parents had brought him up with a commitment to public service and philanthropy. As a child, he had watched as his father wrote out a check to the National Association for the Advancement of Colored People, then the leading civil rights organization in America. When he asked why his father had picked them, his father explained that discrimination against one group was discrimination against all groups. One of Mike's first acts of philanthropy was to endow a chair at Harvard Business School in his father's name.

Our initial polling gave Bloomberg only a faint chance of being elected mayor. We estimated the odds at just one-in-three. I actually took it on myself to try to talk him out of running for mayor. I'm proud I did so for honesty's sake, at the potential cost to my own business, but in retrospect I'm sure glad that I did not succeed.

Bloomberg made it very clear to me from the get-go that he had his own priorities and would not be driven by our polling. I had two reactions. My first was a twinge of disappointment because as a pollster you want to be more rather than less involved. But at the same time I had an enormous degree of pride and admiration that he was both so independent and willing to be divorced from the political process.

He insisted on running a positive campaign with a focus on the issues. To him, the top issue was education—or rather the lack of it—even though the polls said it was not high up the list of the public's concerns. He had a little speech that went like this: "Every day, I have to wake up and look at myself in the mirror and be proud of what I see. You should never ask me to do anything that would compromise that perception."

Though it began as a long-shot, a set of extraordinary circumstances—which we will revisit later—propelled Bloomberg into City Hall. His principled pursuit of what he perceived to be the public interest, and his personal wealth, meant that he was literally elected without owing anybody anything. That is a rarity in politics. In three terms as mayor, he pushed through initiatives that he felt were right, even if they were not popular. He raised taxes to close the budget deficit, reformed the public schools, and instituted a widely copied indoor smoking ban that has saved hundreds of thousands if not millions of lives.

I later asked Bloomberg what had surprised him most when he entered politics. His reply was, how limited most politicians are and how so few genuinely care about the broader public interest.

CHARLES EVERS

Mayor of Fayette, Mississippi 1985-1989, 1969-1981

Charles Evers, right, a former pimp and numbers runner, and brother of the assassinated civil rights activist Medgar Evers, is sworn in on July 7, 1969, as the first Black mayor in Mississippi since Reconstruction.

Truth 7

USE YOUR ANGER

You must be clever with your anger. Rather than a source of rage, it should be a bottomless reservoir of strength and determination that gives you a power others do not share. Outrage is one of the most useful emotions in the world.

A SELF-STYLED HUSTLER, Charles Evers pimped prostitutes and ran his own numbers racket in Chicago in competition with the Mob. He always carried two guns—a .38 pistol and a sawed-off shotgun. When his younger brother was assassinated by a white racist back home in Mississippi, he returned down South determined to kill white people in revenge.

But he didn't do it.

By the time I met him, he had gone into politics instead.

The killing of Medgar Evers, Charles's kid brother, on June 12, 1963, opened an era of political violence in America. Soon President John F. Kennedy, the three "Mississippi Burning" voting-rights activists, Dr. Martin Luther King, and Bobby Kennedy would be dead too—all people Charles Evers knew.

Born in the 1920s, the Evers brothers grew up Black in the segregated South where they could not eat at the same lunch counter, use the same bathroom, or drink from the same water fountain as whites. They had to call whites "ma'am" or "sir" but were always just called the N-word in return. Blacks made up almost 50 percent of the population of their home state of Mississippi but just 4 percent of voters, because whites made it virtually impossible to register to vote. Lynchings were a regular gruesome occurence. Decades after the formal end of slavery, whites could still kill Blacks with impunity.

From the time that Charles was eight and Medgar just five, the brothers vowed to fight for Blacks to get justice. They became admirers of the Mau Mau revolt against the British Empire in Kenya. Indeed, Medgar would name his firstborn son after Mau Mau mastermind and Kenya's first independent leader Jomo Kenyatta. The brothers fantasized about a Mau Mau–style insurrection against the whites in Mississippi. They made a childhood pact that if one of them went down, the other would carry on.

Charles liked to say that Medgar, nicknamed "Lope," was the saint of the family. And he was the loudmouth. While Charles headed north to hustle in the relative freedom of Chicago, Medgar stayed to make his point in Mississippi. In 1954, Medgar decided to challenge the system by applying to study law at "Ole Miss," the all-white state-funded University of Mississippi. Despite the Supreme Court ruling in *Brown vs. Board of Education* desegregating America's schools, Medgar was turned down because he did not have enough white references. His campaign attracted the attention of the National Association for the Advancement of Colored People in New York, then America's leading civil rights group. Despite the risk to life and limb, Medgar signed on to become the NAACP's first-ever field secretary in Mississippi.

"When his younger brother was assassinated by a white racist back home in Mississippi, he returned down South determined to kill white people in revenge."

Racist murders were routine in Mississippi. When Charles was ten and Medgar seven, one of their father's best friends was lynched after it was claimed he had insulted a white woman. Their parents rushed them off the streets when the mob grabbed Willie Tingle. The crowd dragged him through the streets behind a wagon, strung him up from a tree in the meadow, and shot his limp body in half. For days the young boys had to walk past his bloody clothes that were left behind, and it remained with them in their dreams.

As NAACP field secretary it fell to Medgar to investigate the 1955 abduction of fourteen-year-old Emmett Till, accused of flirting with a white woman in Money, Mississippi. When Till's mutilated body floated to the surface of the Mississippi River with one eye missing, Medgar took a photograph. He wanted to galvanize support for Blacks' plight. His investigation forced a trial. But the all-white jury predictably acquitted the killers—who then gave a *Look* magazine interview boasting of the grisly murder. As Medgar hoped, the case became a *cause celebre* that propelled the civil rights struggle into a mass movement.

Fighting on for civil rights in Mississippi, Medgar's home was stoned and firebombed by Ku Klux Klanners. He was threatened, beaten, and shot at. When he returned home from a civil rights rally just after midnight, a white former Marine sharpshooter named Byron De La Beckwith shot him dead with a sniper's rifle.

Charles flew back to Mississippi the next morning in a rage. "I have a sin to admit," he later wrote in his autobiography. "Part of the reason I came back to Mississippi was to kill white folks. At times, in those first months back, I just wanted to kill every white man I could—just kill, kill, kill until a white man struck me down and ended it." He returned to the brothers' childhood "Mau Mau for Mississippi" fantasy, in which he would cruise around the state murdering two prominent racists for every Black killed. Charles had once worked in his father's funeral home. "As a mortician, I knew a lot about how to make men die," he noted.

Happily, Charles used this searing and entirely justified anger for good. Praying each night for God to take away his hate, he came to the conclusion he could best avenge Medgar's death by working for change within the system. He took over Medgar's role at the NAACP, registering Black voters, picketing and boycotting whites-only businesses, and filing lawsuits to integrate schools. In racist town after racist town, the NAACP would deliver a ten-day deadline for the local government to integrate schools and hire Black police officers. Hardest of all to accept for racist whites, he found, was having to call Blacks "mister," "missus," or "miss."

Medgar's murder had brought Charles into contact with President John F. Kennedy. "They'd kill me too," Kennedy told him, "if they could." When President Kennedy was himself assassinated later that year, Charles bonded with Bobby Kennedy over their dead brothers. The two used to visit their brothers' graves together at Arlington National Cemetery, where they both lay. Charles, then campaigning for Bobby to become president, was at the Ambassador Hotel in Los Angeles when Bobby Kennedy was himself assassinated in 1968.

Charles was smart and fiercely independent. For someone who had never played by the rules in the past, he figured out skillfully how to navigate the changing rules of a society in tumult to achieve his goals. In 1969, after a voter registration drive in the small town of Fayette, he was elected the first Black mayor in Mississippi since Reconstruction. Local whites now had to call him not just "mister" but "Mayor Evers."

I met him when, as a first-year Harvard student, I went South with other white activists to help his campaign to become Mississippi governor. He sat us down and lectured us: "Look, guys, this is a new world. This is no longer about guilty white people coming to work for Blacks. I'm the boss. Whatever you think of my past, I've proven I can get on in your world and succeed quite well—and you are in my world now, not your world."

That was the measure in itself of his—and his brother's—achievement. Their righteous anger took them far.

HILLARY RODHAM CLINTON

US Secretary of State 2009-2013, US Senator 2001-2009,
First Lady 1993-2001

Hillary Clinton being comforted by her husband, Bill, after a stage light fell from the ceiling and knocked her down on the set of CBS's 60 Minutes *on Super Bowl Sunday, January 26, 1992. She famously told the show: "I'm not sitting here—some little woman standing by my man like Tammy Wynette."*

Truth 8

DEFINE YOURSELF, YOURSELF

A person can see themselves in many different ways, but it is your responsibility—and should be yours alone—to decide who exactly it is that you wish to present to others.

HILLARY RODHAM SERVED as her husband's First Lady of Arkansas for twelve years. When he was elected president, Hillary Rodham Clinton became First Lady of the United States, then secretary of state, and finally a US senator. In 2016, she ran for the presidency herself—as Hillary Clinton.

Her struggle with her surname reflected the struggle that she, and many of her generation, had with women's evolving identity in the world.

In his winning presidential campaign in 1992, Bill Clinton had rashly promised America a "Buy One, Get One Free" presidency with his wife. Although she would go on to become the first American woman ever to run as a major-party candidate for the presidency, Bill's two-fer offer dogged Hillary's career—and left her with a conflicted identity. Like many women—and an increasing number of men—she struggled to define herself between the sometimes conflicting imperatives of marriage and career. It is a task that is admittedly made infinitely harder if your husband is a philandering president in the full glare of publicity. But she never fully succeeded in defining herself, entirely by herself.

Early on, Bill was a major asset for Hillary, leading her from the Governor's Mansion to the White House to the Senate. By the time of her presidential bid, after several sexual scandals, he hung like a millstone around her neck. When she lost, I'm told by people close to them, Hillary and Bill were for a time not even on speaking terms. She seemed to blame him for her narrow loss.

It was Dick Morris, their longtime pollster, and now their nemesis, who first introduced me to the Clintons in 1995. He explained to me that they had a "push-you-pull-me" marriage. Control see-sawed between them according to circumstance. When Bill made the two-for-one promise to the American electorate in New Hampshire, he surely hoped to appeal to liberal and independent women voters. But Bill always had one audience that he just had to assuage: Hillary.

"It is a task that is admittedly made infinitely harder if your husband is a philandering president in the full glare of publicity."

In that presidential campaign, Hillary saved Bill's bacon. When *The Star* supermarket tabloid reported Bill had engaged in a twelve-year affair with lounge singer Gennifer Flowers, Hillary played the loyal wife. On Super Bowl Sunday 1992, she appeared on *60 Minutes* to insist: "I'm not sitting here, some little woman standing by my man like Tammy Wynette. I'm sitting here because I love him, and I respect him, and I honor what he's been through and what we've been through together. And you know, if that's not enough for people, then heck—don't vote for him."

This defiant message was Hillary's first introduction to most Americans. It rescued Bill's presidential bid. If she had not stuck with him, he would undoubtedly have lost. But it came at a devastating long-term cost to her. The endemic unpopularity that cost her the presidency in her own right in 2016 dates back to that Super Bowl Sunday almost a quarter of a century earlier. That appearance sitting next to her husband in a Boston hotel suite robbed her of the chance to ever define herself purely on her own terms.

In their see-sawing marriage, however, Hillary's *60 Minutes* rescue act put her temporarily in command. When they entered the White House, Bill placed her in charge of his campaign priority: healthcare reform. It was a disaster. When I first met them, Bill was back on top.

In the summer of 1995, a small group of us political advisers were sitting in the president's private study in the White House when Hillary came in. Bill invited her to join in. She looked at him and said: "Bill, you know my political instincts are terrible. You know I always get these things wrong. I'll leave you and your political advisers to sort it out." Bill gallantly countered: "Nonsense, Hillary. We would love to get your insights." But she cried off again. "No, no, no, I'm invariably wrong. You deal with your political advisers." It was an interaction that made clear that at that moment he was in the superior position.

That balance remained through the 1996 election until the Monica Lewinsky scandal broke in 1998. Once again, I was in the White House meeting with Bill, this time tête-à-tête, when Hillary interrupted us. The contrast was telling. Hillary announced that she was going to walk their dog, Buddy. "Oh no, Hillary," Bill said disingenuously, "I'll walk the dog." Again, Hillary refused to join the meeting. "I'll walk him," she insisted. "You are with your political adviser. You're too busy." Bill tried one more time. "Nonsense, I have plenty of time," he insisted. But Hillary was having none of it. "No, I don't want to disturb you at all. I'll walk the dog!" The sub-rosa dialogue was that Bill had got himself in this Lewinsky mess and it was up to him to get out of it. Or, as Hillary might have thought to herself: *I'll deal with the literal doggie doo-doo. You are in far-greater metaphorical doggie doo-doo.*

I think it is clear that had Hillary come out publicly to denounce her husband over the Lewinsky affair, she would have cost him the presidency. He would not have been acquitted at his impeachment trial in the Senate.

Hillary, of course, knew and knows her husband better than anybody else. I knew something was up with Lewinsky in February 1998, because he told me. If I knew, I'm sure Hillary must have known by then too. Other women, such as Paula Jones, to be followed shortly by campaign volunteer Kathleen Willey, were also making sexual allegations against Bill. A large part of Hillary's outrage, I believe, was not the surreptitious sex but the further humiliation it heaped on her.

There is a popular view among Hillary's supporters that, without being shackled to Bill, she could have been president. Already in Bill's first campaign, their friend Linda Bloodworth-Thomason told *Vanity Fair*, "Hillary doesn't have to stay with Bill Clinton. She could get to the Senate or possibly the White House on her own—and she knows it." This has bred a feminist revenge fantasy in which Hillary ditches Bill and becomes president in his stead. This wish-fulfillment drove Curtis Sittenfeld's novel *Rodham*, published after Hillary's 2016 presidential defeat, to the top of the bestseller lists. Its counter-factual premise is that Hillary dumped Bill after moving with him to Arkansas on the first hint of sexual misconduct—the fictional claim by a parking lot attendant that he raped her. Bill's political career implodes when he is accused of a long-term affair with a lounge singer and his alternative wife bombs in a 60 *Minutes* interview. Bill (spoiler alert) becomes a tech titan while Hillary is elected first senator and then president in 2016.

The trouble with this bestselling alternate history—tellingly titled with Hillary's maiden name—is that it is entirely unrealistic. Had Hillary in fact been "liberated" from Bill in this way, she would never have been elected to Daniel Patrick Moynihan's old Senate seat in New York, and therefore would never have become a presidential candidate—and she knows it.

I was Senator Moynihan's pollster and he told me he was planning to retire. Again, if I knew that, surely Hillary, then First Lady, knew it too. She understood that but for her subjugating her ego to Bill, she would not advance. The reason she had to stay with him during the Lewinsky scandal was that she understood that Senator Moynihan was not going to run again and she knew she needed Bill to get that Senate seat. Whatever she may have said, or whatever her supporters believe, her interests were always very clearly aligned with staying with Bill. And that was always her dilemma.

To my mind, Hillary was always looking for a practical path to power without having a vision of what her path should be. Despite her oft-stated commitment to women and children, she seemed to have no bedrock political philosophy. She had seen how Bill won re-election in 1996 as a centrist. When she first ran for the Democratic nomination for president in 2008, she therefore ran as a centrist. She was outflanked by Barack Obama on both the Left, as an activist, and in the middle, as a self-proclaimed unifier of Red America and Blue America. So, when she ran for president again in 2016, she ran to the Left to fend off the challenge from Bernie Sanders in the Democratic primary. That made it harder for her to win over the middle ground in the general election, costing her the presidency.

Hillary did not have the protean political talent of her husband—and she knew that too. She was always fighting the last war. Or perhaps it would be more accurate to say that she was always fighting the war within herself.

SILVIO BERLUSCONI

Prime Minister of Italy 2008–2011, 2001–2006, 1994–1995

Left: Silvio Berlusconi greets Mara Carfagna, the former model and Miss Italy contestant he named as his Equalities Minister in 2008.

Right: Carfagna in her beauty-queen days in the 1997 Miss Italy pageant.

When Berlusconi told Carfagna at a TV awards dinner that he would marry her immediately if he were not already married, his wife wrote to a newspaper to demand he apologize. It was later alleged the two had a two-and-a-half year affair.

Truth 9

BE HAPPY, BE POPULAR

Charisma is a priceless personal attribute. Perhaps it cannot be learned, but that does not mean we cannot understand what it is. It is above all the ability to put others at ease. Etymologically, it derives from the Ancient Greek χαίρω: "I am happy."

THE FIRST TIME I met Silvio Berlusconi I immediately understood why he catapulted to the top of Italian politics to become the country's longest-serving prime minister since Fascist dictator Benito Mussolini. He was funny. He was warm. He had a common touch. With greased-back hair that made him look like an Italian B-movie clown, he was a compelling personality. He was also anti-systemic, having come from outside Italy's entrenched political caste. In short, he had that X Factor: charisma.

Berlusconi worked as a young man in the 1950s as a cabaret singer on cruise ships. Later in life, he would even record two albums and write the anthems for both his soccer team AC Milan and his Forza Italia political movement. Cruise ship crooning was, he once explained to me, how he learned to charm people. "If they didn't like me, it was a long time till we made land and I could get off," he observed.

Of all the world leaders I have met, Berlusconi is the only one who has ever told me that one of his top priorities was having a good time. Most politicians insist on strategizing about how to use every moment, including the Thanksgiving and Christmas holidays, to socialize with donors and others they believe can help them. Berlusconi was the exact opposite. Rarely was he seen without an entourage of beautiful women, many of whom he chose for political positions. As prime minister, he named a former topless model, Mara Carfagna, to be his equalities minister. Even when he was running the country, he was notoriously staying up late for "bunga bunga" sex parties.

"Of all the world leaders I have met, Berlusconi is the only one who has ever told me that one of his top priorities was having a good time."

Berlusconi, along with Reagan, was among the first of a line of elected leaders who acted less as politicians and more as entertainers. After all, he comes from the land where the Ancient Roman poet Juvenal first recognized that all it took to please the public was "bread and circuses." Now it is no longer a surprise that a showman like Boris Johnson or a Reality TV star like

Donald Trump can win power. Berlusconi understood that his own evident enjoyment of life was infectious.

Charisma begins at home. People who are happy within themselves exude contentment and implicitly invite others to share in the fun. It is a good test of charisma to ask whether this or that politician is a happy person. For instance, is the charisma-free Hillary Clinton, the jilted wife who stood by her man, the frustrated healthcare reformer, who had to play second-string as secretary of state after losing the Democratic nomination to Barack Obama, and then lost the presidency to Donald Trump, a happy person? Is her charismatic husband, Bill, a happy person? Well, exactly.

Berlusconi is indubitably a happy person, not troubled by self-doubt. I worked for him when he was prime minister for the second time in the run-up to the 2006 general election. Rather than moving into the prime minister's official residence in Palazzo Chigi, he ran the country from his own palatial home nearby, Palazzo Grazioli—later rumored to be the scene of some of his "bunga bunga" parties.

Berlusconi typically arrived late at our strategy sessions. At one mid-morning meeting, he turned up wet-headed just out of the shower. About half an hour later, a tall blonde woman in a sequined dress slunk into the room. She also had wet hair. To everyone else's discomfort, he invited her to join the discussion. Although he preferred to communicate in Italian through his female translator, Berlusconi could speak perfectly serviceable English. He broke into English to introduce his companion: "Meet my newest MP," the prime minister declared.

When the meeting wrapped up, Berlusconi—addressed by everyone as *Il Presidente*—asked me to take his new muse to lunch with the group. I, of course, agreed. We went around the corner to a hole-in-the-wall, with her still in her sequined dress. She was clearly embarrassed. At one point, she looked at me and said: "I look ridiculous, don't I?" It was clear to me that she had traded a weekend with *Il Presidente* for a spot high up on his party list that would ensure her election to Parliament.

She asked me if I would take her shopping after lunch. Before I could answer, one of Berlusconi's close aides kicked me in the shin under the table. So I cried off, saying I had to work. Every time I tried to discuss anything serious with Berlusconi's blonde colleague, the aide again kicked me in the shins. It was a brutal lunch.

That same evening, we were all invited to a lavish dinner back at Palazzo Grazioli. Berlusconi descended to the pre-dinner cocktails down the grand staircase with the sequin-dressed blonde again on his arm. When she had a chance, she whispered to me: "I still look ridiculous, don't I?"

Berlusconi told me he had two principles in life. One was the defense of liberty. Indeed, he complained that one of his great regrets was that because of his pleasure-loving lifestyle he was not given enough credit for his defense of liberty in Italy and around the world. For him, liberty seemed to have the extra connotation of allowing him to be a libertine. Because his second principle—or should that be his first?—was to enjoy life.

At the dinner, Berlusconi delivered a short speech about how we Americans worked too hard. "You guys don't know how to live," he exhorted us. "Enjoy life. Enjoy women. Your priorities are wrong." It is not something you would ever hear an American politician say—even if they privately believed it—but it would have gone down great with a crowd of hedonistic cruise-ship passengers.

He lost the 2006 election narrowly, but would come back as *Il Presidente* again two years later for a third time.

PART TWO

EVALUATE YOUR CIRCUMSTANCES

None of us live in a void. Before we act,

we must accurately assess the world

around us.

JOE BIDEN

President of the United States 2021–, Vice-President of the United States 2009–2017, US Senator 1973–2009,

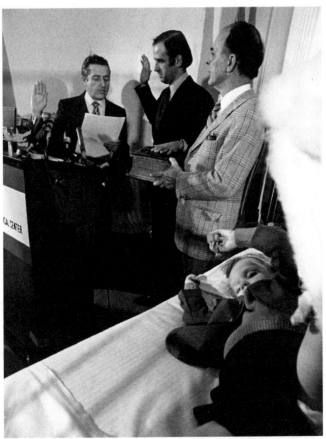

Joe Biden was sworn in as a US senator at a hospital where his injured four-year-old son Beau was being treated, after his wife and baby daughter were killed in a car accident. Mr. Biden's father, Robert Hunter, holds the Bible.

Truth 10

SUCK IT UP

We live in a "grievance culture" that encourages self-pity. Do not feel sorry for yourself. Everyone successful I have ever met has had the resilience to press ahead despite what Shakespeare, already 400 years ago, called "the slings and arrows of outrageous fortune."

JUST SIX WEEKS AFTER Joe Biden won a stunning victory in his first US Senate race, disaster struck. On December 18, 1972, his wife, Neilia, was driving their three children to buy a Christmas tree when she pulled out from a stop sign near Hockessin, Delaware, and was broadsided by a tractor-trailer. The Biden family station wagon was shunted along the highway for 150 feet before plunging backward down an embankment and hitting three trees. Neilia and thirteen-month-old Naomi died. Hunter, two, suffered a fractured skull; Beau, three, had so many broken bones he was put in a full body cast.

For Biden, it was a devastating reversal of fortune. Shortly after his upset Senate win, he had celebrated his thirtieth birthday—making him constitutionally eligible to take up his Senate seat. After the car crash, he considered abandoning his political career before it had really begun, to devote himself to his young boys. "Delaware can get another senator," he told friends, "but my boys can't get another father." He moved into the Wilmington Medical Center to be with them—and it was in the hospital, not in the Senate chamber, that Biden was finally sworn into office.

The forty-sixth US president has been described as the luckiest and the unluckiest of politicians. His father taught him that luck averages out over a lifetime, which necessarily means that the higher the highs, the lower the lows. Whether or not his father's theory is true, Biden has certainly had more than a usual share of both. We will look later—in "Prepare for Luck"—at how Biden has managed his good fortune. Here we will learn from the way he has handled his bad luck.

"After the car crash, he considered abandoning his political career before it had really begun, to devote himself to his young boys."

In his memoir, *Promises to Keep*, Biden imparts another of his father's homespun maxims: Get up! "To me, this is the first principle of life, the foundational principle, and a lesson you can't learn at the feet of any wise man: Get up! The art of living is simply getting up after you've been knocked down," he writes.

Following the car crash, Biden came under heavy pressure from his Democratic colleagues not to abandon the Senate. With his sister and campaign manager, Val, taking care of his boys, he agreed to try it for six months. He ended up serving thirty-six years as a senator, and presided over the Senate for a further eight years as vice president. Yet the landmarks in his long Senate career were not his political successes. They were his personal catastrophes.

During his failed 1988 presidential campaign, Biden started getting searing headaches and kept his schedule by popping six, eight, or even ten Tylenols a day. After collapsing in a Rochester hotel room, he was diagnosed with a brain aneurysm. His second wife, Jill, walked into his hospital room to find a priest giving him the last rites. When surgeons at Walter Reed Medical Center operated, they warned him he could suffer permanent brain damage.

In 2015, his son Beau, the little boy he had tended in the hospital, who grew up to be an Iraq war vet and state attorney general, died of a brain tumor at age forty-six. The death of his oldest son persuaded Biden not to run for president in 2016. Beau was the apple of his eye. "Amtrack Joe" Biden had commuted to Washington by train daily during his Senate career to be with Beau and Hunter in Wilmington when they were children. Before his cancer, Beau was considering a run to become Delaware governor. He had been seen as a rising star of the Democratic Party. Introducing his father when he was nominated as vice president at the 2008 Democratic Convention, Beau was brought to tears recounting his father's focus on raising his surviving kids after the accident.

Biden says he first learned to understand others' personal struggles because he suffered from a stutter as a child. Other kids nicknamed him "Dash"—not because he was fast on the football field but because he spoke like Morse Code. A nun who taught him at Catholic grade school mocked him as "Mr. Bu-Bu-Bu-Bu-Biden." His father taught him not to indulge in self-pity. Indeed, he managed to turn his personal tragedy into a political asset. Even Kitty Kelley, the queen of the journalistic takedown, wrote in *Washingtonian* magazine in 1974 that Biden "reeked of decency." As Beau Biden's Democratic convention speech demonstrated, he made empathy his brand.

Biden is not only able to "suck it up" himself but has an unusual ability to "suck it up" for others, too, with a compassion that he communicates to a broader audience. That has been his calling card. Despite his well-known gaffes (he once boasted: "Folks, I can tell you I've known eight presidents, three of them intimately.") and despite him being something of a blowhard, there is almost no one on Capitol Hill who doesn't like Biden. He finally won the presidency because his empathy contrasted so sharply with the careless callousness of Donald Trump in the coronavirus pandemic. Biden used both the car crash and Beau's death in a campaign ad on TV. "Healthcare is *personal* to me," he declared. Amid the mass bereavement, Biden was elected to be the nation's "Mourner-in-Chief."

THE LIKELY VOTER

The polls were wrong! Harry Truman mocks the Chicago Tribune's front page on November 3, 1948, after beating Thomas Dewey to win the presidential election the previous day.

Truth 11

THE WORLD IS EVERYTHING THAT IS SAID AND DONE...

Listen carefully to everything people say and watch carefully everything they do. It is essential to understand them by their logic, not your own, even if their actions appear absurd or extreme. Only then will you learn how to influence them.

IF YOU WANT TO KNOW what another person is going to do, the simplest way to find out is just to ask them.

That is the basic idea of polling, my business for the last half century.

Only when you understand how they think will you be in a position to persuade them.

But of course it is not always as easy as that. You have to know whom to ask; what to ask them, and when; how to judge the strength of their feelings; and to be able to assess their answers—as well as their non-answers. That is the absorbing, and constantly developing science of opinion polling.

The ultimate goal for a political campaign is to determine who is a "likely voter" and what you need to do to win their support. It is, however, also a good model to pursue in your own private life. Understand your circumstances before you act. In politics, the first survey of a campaign is called the "benchmark poll." Understand your own "benchmark" circumstances.

"Some taverns put out 'poll books' for patrons to jot down their voting preference, whether sober or not."

The first "straw polls" in American democracy date all the way back to 1824, the first contested presidential election in US history that was supposed to be decided largely by the popular vote. In the end, of course, it was not: The House of Representatives stepped in to hand the presidency to John Quincy Adams even though he got a smaller share of the popular vote and fewer Electoral College votes than Andrew Jackson. But the fact that eighteen out of the twenty-four states then chose their electors by a popular vote, rather than by caucuses—twinned with the fact that it was the first competitive race since 1800—meant the public craved advance knowledge of who the winner would be. During the campaign, unscientific "straw polls" were held at militia musters, political rallies, jury calls, in barrooms, and even aboard ships. Some taverns put out "poll books" for patrons to jot down their voting preference, whether sober or not. The results were published by local newspapers. On October 8, the *Star and North Carolina Gazette* aggregated the results of fifty-five of these deeply flawed straw polls in a pioneering "poll of polls."

Newspaper editors had long relied on trusted local figures and public endorsements to judge the election "horse-race"—as we still do today. Over the course of the nineteenth century and into the twentieth century, however, the newspapers took on the task of conducting polling themselves. The most famous was launched by the *Literary Digest* in 1916, partly as a circulation gimmick. The *Literary Digest* mailed out millions of postcards asking voters to fill them in and return them for their favored candidate. The weekly correctly predicted the victories of Woodrow Wilson in 1916, Warren Harding in 1920, Calvin Coolidge in 1924, Herbert Hoover in 1928, and Franklin Delano Roosevelt in 1932. In the 1936 race, it mailed out 10 million postcards to its readers and registered owners of telephones and automobiles. Some 2.27 million potential voters replied—a simply enormous number by current polling standards. The respondents gave Republican Kansas governor Alfred Landon a crushing lead of 55 to 41 percent over President Roosevelt. "The Poll represents the most extensive straw ballot in the field—the most experienced in view of its twenty-five years of perfecting—the most unbiased in view of its prestige—a Poll that has always previously been correct," the weekly crowed. When the actual election took place, however, Roosevelt won by a landslide 61 to 37 percent, taking forty-six of the forty-eight US states (Alaska and Hawaii became states later). Its credibility shot, the million-selling *Literary Digest* collapsed soon afterward.

The new boys on the polling block did, however, call the winner accurately in 1936. George Gallup, Elmo Roper, and Archibald Crossley had used scientific sampling of much smaller numbers. These new techniques had been imported into politics from the commercial world, where they were developed for market research to establish a product's appeal and market share. Success was particularly sweet for Crossley, who had once worked as research director for the *Literary Digest*.

Subsequent studies showed that, by focusing on its own readers and automobile- and telephone-owners, the *Literary Digest* had skewed its sample toward Republicans. What's more, anti-Roosevelt voters felt more strongly about the incumbent president than anti-Landon voters did against the pretender, and were thus more likely to send their postcards back—a phenomenon known in the business as "response bias." The truth is that you can be more predictive with a random sample of 1,000 in a country of 150 million, as the United States then was, than with a biased response of 2 million plus.

The Gallup Poll went on to become the gold standard. But George Gallup got his comeuppance too. In 1948, his polling predicted Republican Thomas Dewey would defeat Democrat Harry Truman by 5 to 15 percentage points. Gallup, however, made the lethal mistake of ending his polling three weeks before the election. "Give 'em Hell, Harry" Truman went negative, attacking the "Do-Nothing Congress," and surged to a four-and-a-half-point victory.

If I may say so modestly, this is where, in the history of polling, I come in. As a freshman at Harvard in the early 1970s, I looked up to a twenty-one-year-old senior named Pat Caddell, one of the new generation of polling pioneers. I freely admit I was jealous. I was still basically a *schlepper* handing out election flyers in East Harlem or Mississippi. From his dorm room, Caddell was already running a national polling business and being courted by Democratic senators.

Caddell pioneered polling on the alienation Americans felt as a result of racial divisions and the Vietnam War. He was the first to systematically understand that you could use polling to shape and frame attitudes. He introduced the element of *persuasion* into polling.

I was even younger than Caddell, but I could see that his approach was the future of the politics business. In 1976, Caddell proved that to be correct: At the age of just twenty-six, he helped Georgia peanut-farmer-cum-governor Jimmy Carter win a long-shot bid for the presidency.

In the mayoral contest in New York the following year—which I will write about in the chapter on "Distract and Mislead"—I found myself facing off against Caddell. I was working for Democratic contender Ed Koch; Caddell for rival Democrat Mario Cuomo. It was in this contest that I made my own first major innovation in polling. The dominant pollsters, like Gallup, had traditionally collected information by going door-to-door in selected neighborhoods. But by the 1970s, more than 95 percent of Americans had telephones. Simply by calling every tenth voter on the registration rolls, or by calling randomly generated numbers, you could get a representative sample. With my partner Mark Penn, we set up a room of survey-takers and gave them numbers to call. Armed with telephone polling and a new micro-computer, we were able to tabulate survey results as they came in. (Now it is all done automatically.) This "overnight polling" gave us the edge, because time, as we have seen, is of the essence in decisionmaking. Several decades later, Caddell and I would do a weekly TV show together, *Political Insiders*.

Working for Clinton in the 1996 campaign, Penn and I came up with a second major innovation, once again imported from the commercial world. We started to assess voters' *values* by asking them about such hot-button issues as abortion, gay rights, school prayer, and the American flag. The results gave Clinton the insight to launch a series of values-based initiatives, aligning himself with the majority of American families.

I took this approach further when working for Michael Bloomberg on his first run to become mayor of New York in 2000. Bloomberg, a tech wizard himself, favored a data-driven approach. Compiling information on individual New York voters, we were able to build a comprehensive model of the city electorate online, years before Barack Obama's 2008 presidential campaign did the same. As with Koch, our technical advance propelled us to victory.

It is an unfortunate fact of life that most people don't listen, won't listen, and can't listen. Don't be one of them. Learn the lesson of my polling career. If you listen carefully, other people will tell you what they are thinking and what they are going to do. You may find their views objectionable or even bizarre. But you'll be surprised how much you can learn just by paying attention to the words they use.

THE "SHY TRUMPER"

A Trump supporter gets into his truck after hearing Republican presidential candidate Donald Trump speak at the Living History Farms Visitor Center in Urbandale, Iowa, January 15, 2016.

Truth 12

...AND THE WORLD IS EVERYTHING THAT IS NOT SAID AND NOT DONE

We comfortably assume that people choose to say what they say and choose to do what they do. We should equally assume that they choose what they do *not* say and do *not* do. Our mothers taught us: "If you have nothing good to say, say nothing." We cannot accurately evaluate the world unless we take into account everything people choose *not* to say and choose *not* to do. It is the "dark matter" of the universe of free will.

IN THE FINAL DAYS of the 2016 US presidential race, the *New York Times* estimated that Hillary Clinton had as much as a 91 percent chance of winning. The newspaper helpfully explained that her risk of losing was the same as the probability of an NFL kicker missing a 31-yard field goal. The *Huffington Post* put Clinton's chances at 98 percent. The Princeton Election Consortium estimated her victory was an all but inevitable 99 percent.

Well, as we all know, Hillary missed the field goal. All hail, President Trump.

In the months before that election, I wrote that momentum favored Trump and that Clinton's election was not a shoo-in. In the final days, I estimated Clinton's odds at around 60 percent. So, although I gave Trump much better odds than most, my polling still made Hillary the odds-on winner.

So what went wrong?

The problem is multifaceted — but the biggest single factor is that Trump voters don't say what they are going to do. Although Trump himself is a loudmouth, and many of his supporters are even louder, this has become known in my business as the problem of the "Shy Trumper." The problem for me as a pollster — and for everyone in everyday life — is how to read a person's intentions if they refuse to say what they are going to do.

The problem first burst into public view in Florida in the 2000 presidential election, when it became a life-threatening issue for our republic. Exit polling gave the decisive state — and hence the entire election — to Al Gore. The Voter News Service, the television networks' exit polling consortium, called Florida for Gore shortly before 8:00 p.m., only to retract its prediction two hours later. In fact, the Supreme Court found that George W. Bush won by 537 votes out of almost 6 million — a margin of 0.00009 percent.

It has become increasingly clear since then that many conservative Republicans feel alienated from the political establishment and the mainstream media — and refuse to talk openly with pollsters. The problem for pollsters only became worse with the arrival of political outsider Trump. Many Republicans were frankly embarrassed to admit to strangers that they were voting for Trump. Hence, "Shy Trumpers."

For us pollsters, the problem is compounded by the increasing difficulty of getting a representative sample. If a voter is alienated from the system, and thinks the game is rigged, and the swamp needs to be drained, they are less likely to answer our phone call. Add to that the technological transformation of our society, and it throws the whole polling business—the business I have spent my life in—into serious question. When I first developed overnight telephone polling for New York mayoral candidate Ed Koch in the 1977 campaign, I could be confident that someone with a telephone would pick up and answer questions. Now, many young people only use their phones for texting, tweeting, and social media, or communicate through encrypted apps like WhatsApp or Snapchat. The lesson for pollsters—and all of us in our everyday lives—is to pay attention to what others say and do, in all spheres, and draw inferences about their silences from that. Pay attention to them *holistically*.

Nowadays, we supplement our traditional telephone polling with inquiries about voters' values and try to coax answers from "shy" voters by asking indirect questions. After getting an evasive answer to a straight question about whether a voter is going to support Trump, for example, we might ask, "Do any of your family and friends like Trump?" "Will any of your family and friends vote for Trump?" "Can you understand why they will vote for Trump?" An "undecided" voter who answers "yes" to such questions is overwhelmingly likely to vote for Trump, even though they refuse to say so.

"If I know your positions on eight or ten issues, I can infer with 95 percent certainty what you think about everything."

As well as just talking to voters, we now also use data analytics to study their behavior, from their shopping habits to their membership in voluntary associations. One of the best predictors of voting intention, for instance, is churchgoing. You do not have to be a political genius to realize that if you are white and go to church regularly, you are more likely to vote Republican; and if you do yoga, you lean, so to speak, Democrat. If you subscribe to Harley-Davidson's *The Enthusiast* magazine, you are probably Republican. If you read *Mother Jones*, you are a Democrat.

Increasingly, if I know your positions on eight or ten issues, I can infer with 95 percent certainty what you think about everything. I can infer what you think, I can infer what you do, I can infer how you live. And if I throw in a few magazine subscriptions, and which TV programs you watch, and what you do on social media, and where you pray, I know everything there is to know about you—including how you will vote in the sanctity of the polling booth,

Now that you know that about me, do try it yourself at home.

ANTHONY WEINER

US Representative 1999–2011

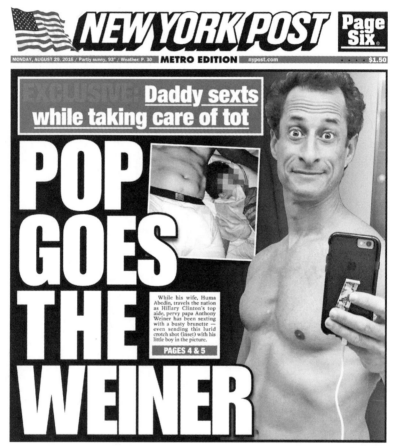

Disgraced congressman Anthony Weiner "sexted" an image of himself lying in bed next to his son to a forty-something divorcee. "You do realize you can see you[r] Weiner in that pic??" the woman texted back.

Truth 13

PEOPLE ARE NOT NORMAL

You make a fatal error if you assume that other people are just like you. They are not. They are weird—even if you cannot tell so from outside. Pay full attention to those around you. If something does not sound right, figure out why.

I FIRST ENCOUNTERED Anthony Weiner when I was working for New York mayor Michael Bloomberg, a nominal Republican. Weiner was a Democratic mayoral challenger. We ran into each other several times in the "Green Room" backstage at Fox News. To my bafflement, Weiner would just start gratuitously insulting me. Even as a New Yorker, I am not used to being abused by total strangers—and I have never been spontaneously harassed like that by any other well-known public figure.

Weiner's insults were more strange than offensive. He struck me as a little weird—but I certainly didn't realize how weird. It was only later that I and the rest of the world came to know that this prominent politician had a secret online life as "Carlos Danger."

Mayor Bloomberg's campaign manager, Bradley Tusk, had a similar intuition that not all was right with Weiner. Weiner, then a New York congressman, had run against Bloomberg in the 2005 mayoral race and was the leading challenger early in the 2009 campaign. Tusk was convinced that if we just did some "oppo research"—a topic we will revisit in a later chapter— Weiner would self-destruct. So when Tusk heard Weiner was an ice hockey freak, he decided to go in person to the Chelsea Piers rink to see if Weiner was playing his weekly game with friends when he should have been voting in Congress on a Thursday night. Of course, he was—playing goal for his beloved amateur Falcons team. It turned out he had missed a series of votes in Congress. As the *New York Post* put it, he was playing hooky to play hockey. Another thing that was a little weird about Weiner.

Still, nobody knew the true extent of his weirdness—until late on Friday night, May 27, 2011.

A selfie photo of a man's gray underpants containing a bulging erection popped up on Weiner's Twitter feed to his 45,000 followers. The congress-man, who had just been tweeting about hockey, deleted the crotch shot moments later. At first, he claimed he had been hacked. "When your name is Weiner, it goes with the territory," he joked on CNN. Within days, however, he had to admit to his newly pregnant wife and the grossed-out general public that he had mistakenly posted what was meant to be a private direct message to his Twitter feed himself.

Perhaps understandably, even his pregnant wife could not fully appreciate the problem. Huma Abedin, a close aide of then–secretary of state Hillary

Clinton, was a devout Muslim raised in Saudi Arabia who had married her first love as a thirty-four-year-old virgin. "This behavior seemed so outside of Anthony's DNA that I was sure it was just a weird blip," she thought. The couple went to crisis therapy at a Texas clinic. When the psychotherapists suggested Weiner had some "narcissist issues," his closest adviser shrugged. "Seriously?" she said. "Doesn't that describe every politician on the planet?"

"When the psychotherapists suggested Weiner had some 'narcissist issues,' his closest adviser shrugged. 'Seriously?' she said. 'Doesn't that describe every politician on the planet?'"

Weiner, a seven-term congressman, admitted he had been "sexting" six women and resigned from the House of Representatives days later.

After therapy and patching up his marriage, and the birth of his son, Jordan, a supposedly reformed Weiner decided to make a comeback bid for New York mayor in the 2013 campaign. He asked New Yorkers to "give me a second chance."

Midway through campaigning, however, new "sexts" came out. Weiner had been exchanging dirty talk with at least three women online under the unforgettable alias "Carlos Danger." One of those women, Sydney Leathers, explained that she had gone into the porn business because her real name already made people assume she was a porn star. She said Weiner accurately described himself to her as "an argumentative, perpetually horny, middle-aged man." Even after Huma stood by her husband Hillary Clinton–style at a press conference, New Yorkers decided unsurprisingly not to give Weiner a second chance. He got under 5 percent of the vote.

Weiner's weirdness took an even more sinister turn in 2016. First, a new "crotch shot" emerged showing him in white underwear with a visible erection with his toddler, Jordan, next to him in bed. For Huma, the appearance of their child was the final straw. She announced their immediate separation.

The following month, it was reported that Weiner had been "sexting" a fifteen-year-old high school student in North Carolina. "I would bust that tight p—y so hard and so often that you would leak and limp for a week," Weiner wrote on the instant message app Kik under the handle "T Dog." Weiner's laptop was seized by police to search for child pornography. With just eleven days to go before the 2016 presidential election, the FBI chief, James Comey, announced that some of Hillary Clinton's emails had been found on the computer. The FBI intervention gave a last-minute boost to Donald Trump. The FBI quickly concluded no classified material was compromised. But Weiner's "sexting" may have cost Hillary Clinton the presidency.

Weiner was convicted of transferring obscene material to a minor and served fifteen months in prison. Ever since, he has been required to register as a sex offender. Those random insults in the Green Room that seemed strange and erratic to me had in fact been an early sign of a much deeper psychodrama that arguably changed world history by putting Trump in the White House and costing America its first woman president.

ASHRAF GHANI
President of Afghanistan 2014–2021,
and
JOE BIDEN

President Ashraf Ghani offered me a job in Afghanistan. I'm glad I turned him down. It didn't end well. US forces fled from Kabul airport. I might have been on that plane—if I was lucky.

Truth 14

THINK
WITHOUT HOPE

Hope can be a great motivator, but it is also a great peril. Countless are those who anticipate the outcome they hope for, rather than the outcome they can rationally expect. Whenever you catch yourself hoping, try a little mind game of thinking things through without hope. You will find it saves you many mistakes.

AT A TWO-HOUR LUNCH at the Harvard Club in New York, Afghanistan's president, Ashraf Ghani, invited me to become an adviser to his US-backed government in Kabul. Ghani is an Americanized anthropologist and former World Bank official who went to high school for a year in Oregon, got his PhD from Columbia University, and taught at Berkeley and Johns Hopkins. He seemed very committed and his offer very sincere. But I'm very happy I turned down his offer—otherwise I might not be here to write to you today.

First, the five-star Kabul hotel where he suggested I live was attacked by Taliban gunmen targeting foreigners, sparking a twelve-hour battle that left forty people dead. Then his government was abandoned by the United States and, as US troops made a chaotic retreat leaving many Americans behind, Ghani himself had to flee the country with two minutes' notice.

It is a deeply unedifying sight to see an American president close his eyes, cross his fingers and toes, touch wood, and hope for the best.

Yet this seems to have been the Afghanistan policy of successive US administrations, particularly President Biden, a supposed foreign policy "expert."

"It is a deeply unedifying sight to see an American president close his eyes, cross his fingers and toes, touch wood, and hope for the best."

As a pollster, I completely recognize the American public's exhaustion with what was dubbed "The Forever War." The post-9/11 invasion of Afghanistan became the longest war in US history. But we must remember that tens of thousands of US troops have been stationed in Germany and Korea for much, much longer. The Afghan war had been more or less stabilized with a much smaller American force and the use of American air power. By withdrawing entirely, Biden snatched defeat from the jaws of stalemate.

President George W. Bush had ordered the gradual drawdown of US forces from Iraq after trying to stabilize the country with a troop "surge." Even then, US soldiers were forced to return to battle the resurgent Islamic State. President Barack Obama set a similar goal of pulling out of Afghanistan.

President Donald Trump, trying to push off the problem into the future, actually signed up to a Taliban deadline. But President Biden did not have to stick with a withdrawal deadline. Indeed, Trump himself claimed that, if he were in Biden's position, he would not have done so.

A phone call between Biden and Ghani three weeks before the Taliban takeover of Kabul in 2021, later leaked to Reuters, revealed how Biden was focused on the "perception" that the Afghan government was losing the war. "I need not tell you the perception around the world and in parts of Afghanistan, I believe, is that things are not going well in terms of the fight against the Taliban," Biden said. "And there is a need, whether it is true or not, there is a need to project a different picture."

Biden had pushed to pull out from Afghanistan since serving as Obama's vice president, and pigheadedly insisted. He set an artificial deadline not based on any military assessment but to end the conflict before the twentieth anniversary of the 9/11 attacks on September 11, 2021. It was a PR point. When non-essential US diplomats started to leave Kabul in April 2021, the overall US intelligence assessment was reportedly that US-trained Afghan government forces would fend off the Taliban at least another eighteen months. As the deadline approached, that assessment grew grimmer and grimmer. US intelligence agencies' estimate of the Ghani government's life expectancy was cut to six to twelve months, then to ninety days, and eventually to just a month. Yet, just weeks before the final withdrawal, Biden promised America there would be no repeat of the traumatizing US retreat from Vietnam. He had no contingency plan.

In the end, the Taliban just walked into Kabul without a fight in a matter of hours. When he woke up on that day, August 15, 2021, President Ghani had "no inkling" he was about to flee for his life, he later told the BBC. That afternoon, he was waiting for a car to the Defense Ministry when his "terrified" national security adviser burst in and announced he had two minutes to leave. Ghani had given instructions to evacuate to the Afghan city of Khost on the Pakistani border. But Khost had fallen. It was only when his flight took off that he realized he was leaving Afghanistan.

"My life's work has been destroyed," he said from exile in the United Arab Emirates. "My values had been trampled on. And I have been made a scapegoat."

Biden still does not understand how his over-optimistic withdrawal has holed his presidency. The famous image of the last helicopter leaving the US embassy roof in Saigon now has a companion in the TV pictures of crowds running alongside a departing US military transport plane at Kabul airport and falling from it when it took off. The United States, a superpower, was left having to negotiate "safe passage" out of the country with a ragtag guerrilla force. The humiliation signaled American weakness for other theaters from Taiwan to Belarus, Kazakhstan, and Ukraine.

Biden suffered a precipitous drop in the polls after the Afghan withdrawal. While it is true that Americans don't raise Afghanistan in polling, the withdrawal contributed to the popular image of Biden as a weak, elderly, and blundering president. He hoped for the best—ignoring the totally predictable risk—and continues to pay the price.

ALEXANDRIA OCASIO-CORTEZ

US Representative 2019–

Former bartender Rep. Alexandria Ocasio-Cortez (D-NY) returns behind the bar to shake a margarita at the Queensboro Restaurant in Queens, NY, on May 31, 2019.

Truth 15

PIGGYBACK THE STORY

The public gets gripped by trends. It is hard to generate them, but easy to ride them. Make sure you understand the meta-narrative of the moment, and position yourself accordingly. The surefire way to success is to surf the big story.

I KNOW PEOPLE who used to work with Alexandria Ocasio-Cortez when she was a bartender at Flats Fix, a narrow *taqueria* in a former garage just off New York's Union Square. To them, she was just "Sandy from the Bronx"—and was not overtly political. ·

Now she is AOC—known to the whole world by her initials—and is seen by many as the future of American politics. The *New York Times* calls her "a political rock star."

AOC has unquestionable personal charisma—and, as she likes to point out sarcastically, a "symmetrical face." But she is riding a wave of demographic, generational, and cultural change that is much greater than herself. The late-night comedian Trevor Noah welcomed her to *The Daily Show* by saying astutely, "Congratulations on being both the dream of half the country, and a nightmare of another half."

Ocasio-Cortez is the single most potent emblem of a changing America as a young generation that is majority-minority inexorably replaces the predominantly white Baby Boomers born after World War II. She rode the "pink wave" of female candidates in 2018 to become the youngest congresswoman ever, at the age of just twenty-nine.

Her own victory in New York was itself symbolic of these tectonic shifts in the electorate. Volunteered by her younger brother to be a candidate for the Bernie Sanders–inspired group "Brand New Congress," Ocasio-Cortez ran part of her campaign from a paper shopping bag she kept behind the bar at Flats Fix. When she left work she would reach into that bag to grab some campaign leaflets and a change of clothes and head out to canvass. "I'm running because everyday Americans deserve to be represented by everyday Americans," she proclaimed.

Campaigns fueled by generational and demographic change are rare in American politics. John F. Kennedy's election as the youngest US president and the first Catholic in the White House is the prime example, but there is also Eugene McCarthy's unsuccessful bid for the 1968 Democratic presidential nomination at the height of the Vietnam War protests, and Barack Obama's election as America's first Black president. On the Republican side, we saw the "Young Republicans" revolution that produced a cohort of political operatives that included Karl Rove, Paul Manafort, and Roger Stone. The renewed activism of Ocasio-Cortez's generation was ironically triggered by the narrow 2016 victory of Donald Trump—itself a kind of nostalgic revolt by the aging Baby Boomers.

"Ocasio-Cortez is the single most potent emblem of a changing America as a young generation that is majority-minority inexorably replaces the predominantly white Baby Boomers born after World War II."

In Ocasio-Cortez's run, the generational, demographic, and cultural change was visible for all to see. Her opponent in New York had been an elected official since before she was born. Ten-term congressman Joe Crowley served as chairman of the Democratic caucus, making him the fourth most senior Democrat in the House of Representatives. He had not faced a primary challenge in fourteen years. The corpulent fifty-six-year-old Irish American former New York police detective had no idea how to deal with a young female working-class Bronx-born Puerto Rican touting radical ideas—except to ignore her.

Ocasio-Cortez's primary challenge seemed certain to fail. Even her own polling put her down by 35 percentage points. She was running on a Progressive wish-list platform of Medicare-for-All, a $15 minimum wage, tuition-free public college, ending private prisons, and the abolition of the Immigration and Customs Enforcement (ICE) agency that was separating families at the Mexican border. Embracing a label that was long a stigma in American politics, she self-identified as a "Democratic Socialist."

As a political professional, I can tell you that getting people to vote in primaries is one of the most difficult things of all. If you are a registered Democrat and you never vote in primaries, for me to persuade you to actually vote in a primary, when you only vote in general elections, is a Herculean task. For me, Ocasio-Cortez's upset primary win—by a stunning 15 percentage points—showed not that the polling was wrong. It showed, rather, that Ocasio-Cortez had expanded the electoral universe by turning out people who did not vote before.

Despite their polar-opposite politics, Ocasio-Cortez shares this ability to expand the electorate with Trump. With Americans deeply disillusioned with "the system" and cynical about politics, there is little that the mainstream politicians can offer them. This is what the establishment hates most: people they don't know. They can't read them and don't know how to address their concerns. "I think we're scared of things we're not familiar with, that show power," Ocasio-Cortez told *Vogue* magazine. "If a spaceship landed in your backyard, it's like 'What the fuck is that? Is it going to hurt me?'"

Since arriving in Congress, Ocasio-Cortez has teamed up with other newly elected young radical House members to form "The Squad." One of the first things she did was to stage a sit-in in the office of House Speaker Nancy Pelosi. As a representative of a new wave of Progressive politicians, she has pulled the whole Democratic Party to the Left. She is both the beneficiary of a new narrative in American politics and now a writer of it.

ED KOCH

Mayor of New York City 1978–1989

Ed Koch celebrating his 1977 election as mayor of New York with former Miss America Bess Myerson, whom he hinted could become his First Lady—even though he was a homosexual.

Truth 16

DISTRACT AND MISLEAD

It is important to focus other people's attention where you want it to be and to remove it from where you don't want it to be. Other people don't pay you much attention—they have better things to do—so are generally easy to distract and mislead, especially by a sparkling object.

THE POSTERS PASTED along Queens Boulevard in New York put it starkly: "Vote for Cuomo, not the Homo." Ed Koch had a problem. The 1977 campaign was his second run to become New York mayor. His first attempt to run as a Greenwich Village liberal in 1973 had gone nowhere. Now he was chased by whispers about his sexuality.

My polling for Koch showed that the public was not particularly interested in whether Koch was gay or not. But his chief adviser, David Garth, feared the rumors might prove decisive in a tight race, because it was the more conservative outer borough Jewish and Catholic voters who were the key swing voters. So he came up with a genius solution. Her name was Bess Myerson.

The 5'10" daughter of Russian-Jewish immigrants to the Bronx had achieved iconic status when she became the first—and only—Jewish Miss America just days after Japan's surrender ended World War II. As my father endearingly explained to me, she was the heartthrob of every Jewish man of his generation. The director of the pageant had tried to convince her to adopt a stage name that was less "Jewish"—but she had refused. When she won Miss America, some sponsors withdrew and she found "No Jews" signs at some venues as she toured. But she fought back with a six-month lecture tour for the Anti-Defamation League titled: "You Can't be Beautiful and Hate."

Myerson was always more than a bathing-suited beauty. An honors student in music at Hunter College, she played Gershwin's "Summertime" on the flute and parts of Grieg's Concerto on the piano in the talent section of the Miss America pageant. When she won, the announcer declared: "Beauty with brains, that's Miss America of 1945." She was invited to play Rachmaninoff's Second Piano Concerto as a guest soloist with the New York Philharmonic at Carnegie Hall. After nine years modeling mink coats and handing out prizes on the TV game show *The Big Payoff*, Mayor John Lindsay named her New York City's first Consumer Affairs Commissioner.

Myerson was happy to accompany Koch to campaign events, sometimes conspicuously holding hands with him. Neither she nor Koch did anything to dispel speculation that theirs was more than a political relationship. Garth even took the unprecedented step of putting Myerson on a campaign poster alongside Koch. At rallies, Koch asked: "Wouldn't she make a great First Lady of Gracie Mansion?"

Within the campaign, there was never any direct discussion about Koch's sexuality. It was all handled in euphemisms: The rumors were a political problem to be addressed. Koch certainly had his own circle of friends, but none of us knew anything about a male lover—although it later emerged there was one. One friend of mine claimed privately that Koch had put the moves on him, but that was hardly conclusive proof. It was a different time: If Koch had come out as gay, it would almost certainly have cost him the race.

"When Koch insisted 'I am a heterosexual,' the gay rights campaigner Larry Kramer protested with a banner reading 'And I am Marilyn Monroe.'"

Indeed, Koch was the ultimate political chameleon. He was always ready to shed his skin. The son of Jewish immigrants, like Myerson, he began his political career in New York's Greenwich Village as a Reformer challenging the former Tammany Hall boss Carmine DeSapio. He was pro–civil rights, anti-Vietnam, and a vocal early supporter of gay rights. As a young representative from New York, he co-sponsored a gay rights bill in Congress. But when he tried to run for mayor in 1973, he found he could get nowhere with voters or donors as a Greenwich Village liberal.

His nakedly political deal with Myerson, engineered by Garth, was just one of his transformations. He conducted a full-scale overhaul, reinventing himself as what he called "a liberal with sanity." In the 1977 race, our polling initially showed him placing last in the Democratic field. He recast himself to appeal to the outer borough Jews and Catholics he needed: Pro–death penalty—and definitely not gay. He courted the support of the Tammany Hall pols who controlled the Democratic Party machine in Brooklyn and the Bronx, and he struck a deal for support with Rupert Murdoch, the newly arrived conservative proprietor of the *New York Post*.

Koch narrowly won the primary to face a runoff against future New York governor Mario Cuomo. It was Cuomo's nineteen-year-old son, Andrew, whom Koch blamed for the "Vote Cuomo, not the Homo" poster campaign.

In a final salvo, Garth persuaded Myerson to shoot Koch's final thirty-second TV spot. "Whatever happened to character, Mr. Cuomo?" she asked. "We thought your campaign would do better than that."

Koch beat Cuomo to the Democratic nomination by 22 to 21 percent. Cuomo, however, refused to abandon his quest and ran as a Liberal in the November mayoral election. Koch beat him again 50 to 42 percent. At the victory party, Koch and Myerson clasped hands above their heads as the crowd chanted "First Lady Bess."

Koch's seventy-four-year-old father, Louis, apparently playing along, predicted a marriage announcement before Koch's mayoral inauguration. According to biographer, Jennifer Preston, however, Myerson had already met rich private investor J. Gordon Marcus, with whom she soon started an affair. Myerson herself was forced to squelch the rumors that she and Koch had wedding plans. "I must have my privacy," Myerson told a reporter a day after Koch's win.

To this day, Koch is reviled in much of the gay community for running the city from the closet. Passions got extremely high when AIDS ravaged the city. Koch, it is claimed, avoided taking an activist role as mayor in case he was accused of being gay himself. When Koch insisted "I am a heterosexual," the gay rights campaigner Larry Kramer protested with a banner reading "And I am Marilyn Monroe."

Koch, who died in 2013, never confirmed he was gay. The 2009 documentary *Outrage* outed Koch's two-year relationship in the 1970s with a man named Richard Nathan. When Koch won, Nathan had expected a mayoral appointment. Instead, Koch cut him out of his life and pushed him into exile in California, where he later died of AIDS. "Dick was worried about his safety. And Dick did feel that if he went public, he would suffer," his friend and trustee Frederick Hertz said in the film. Koch's on-camera response: "Fuck you!"

In an email to Andy Humm of *Gay City News* in 2011, Koch explained his position: "I don't discuss whether I am heterosexual or homosexual. I simply refuse to legitimatize any questions concerning my sexual orientation. For anyone to respond to the question legitimizes its being asked. So that in the future political organizations could not only ask candidates to state their positions on public issues—which is legitimate—but also request an answer to the question 'Are you straight or gay?' To allow that to occur would drive many public-spirited citizens from running for office."

Today, it would be considered outrageous for a political adviser to tell a gay candidate to run on a program that was hostile to gays and to cover up his sexuality with a "beard" like Myerson. But then Koch was prepared to ignore his sexuality, his life history, even his worldview to get elected. His calculated deception, which began with his fake flirtation with Miss America 1945, won him three four-year terms.

There is an amusing coda to the Koch deception, and a sign of how much times have changed. *Sex and the City* star Cynthia Nixon, a married lesbian, ran for New York governor in 2018 against Mario Cuomo's son Andrew, suspected author of the dirty tricks poster campaign against Koch. Nixon neatly reversed the now-notorious campaign slogan so it became: "Vote for the homo, not for the Cuomo." She lost. The aggressively heterosexual Andrew Cuomo was later ousted amid allegations of sexual harrassment.

RICHARD HOLBROOKE

US Permanent Representative to the United Nations
1999–2001, Balkans envoy 1996–1999

Richard Holbrooke, right, hailed as the leading US diplomat of his generation, told me foreign policy was largely "practical thinking and common sense." Seen here with Yugoslav president Slobodan Milošević, who was later indicted as a war criminal, in Belgrade on March 10, 1999.

Truth 17

APPROACH
THE THRONE

Power is all about *access*, about who can whisper in the

emperor's ear. If you don't have the power yourself, get

close to someone who does.

IN 1997, RICHARD HOLBROOKE arranged to ride with me to Washington on the shuttle from New York. As a US special envoy, he had recently negotiated the Dayton Peace Accords that brought a fragile peace to the Balkans. He wanted to speak directly to President Clinton. But he couldn't get an appointment with the president—so he decided to speak to me instead.

Holbrooke, who died in 2010, was one of America's most storied diplomats and the Dayton Accords were his crowning achievement. "Doug, I gotta tell you something," he said. "They call me a 'genius.' They say I fathered this great deal in Bosnia. I'm very pleased with all the kudos and respect and deference I've got. But foreign policy, it ain't that difficult. There is not much to it. It's mostly practical thinking and common sense—and if you quote me on this I will have to deny I know you."

Despite dialing persistently before we boarded and as soon as we landed, Holbrooke could not reach Secretary of State Madeleine Albright that day. She was apparently not picking up for him. He struggled to reach National Security Adviser Sandy Berger. Finally, he got a foot in the door with Berger's deputy, Jim Steinberg. Pressed for time, and characteristically blunt, he half-ordered me to drop off his luggage at the Four Seasons Hotel, which I obligingly did.

"'. . . and if you quote me on this I will have to deny I know you.'"

Despite his brash manner, Holbrooke befriended me because he knew I had worked in Serbia and, more importantly, that I had regular access to Clinton as one of his political consultants. I always accurately conveyed his messages to Clinton. True to form, there was never any reciprocity. Holbrooke didn't even buy me lunch. The most he did was promise once to put me on the board of the prestigious Council on Foreign Relations. We both knew, as soon as he uttered the words, it was never going to happen. And he never mentioned it again.

Yet, I appreciated Holbrooke's acumen, or bureaucratic street smarts. A veteran in-fighter, he knew that if you cannot reach the person in power yourself you have to reach a person who can. I was, for him, that person. It's all about proximity to the throne.

I used my own access to Clinton in planning his political campaigns to push my own view of Serbia. Since working unsuccessfully to oust Serb strongman Slobodan Milošević in 1992, when he stole the election, I had come to believe that only force would dislodge him. On one occasion in the late 1990s, I took Clinton aside and spoke to him for forty minutes about Serbia. I explained that Milošević was a dictator who walked around wearing a bulletproof vest under his bulky trench coat because he was so scared. To get results, the United States needed to threaten his personal safety, I argued. I recommended Clinton bomb the Belgrade neighborhood where Milošević lived.

On March 24, 1999, NATO forces did finally launch an air campaign against Serbia to counter ethnic cleansing in the breakaway province of Kosovo. The air strikes began tentatively in the mistaken belief that Milošević would quickly withdraw from Kosovo. Once again, I raised Serbia with Clinton—even though it was not my brief. I repeated my conviction that Milošević would only respond to a direct physical threat to his safety.

Before dawn on April 23, 1999, NATO dropped three laser-guided bombs on number 15 Uzička Street in the southern Belgrade suburb of Dedinje, where Milošević and his family lived. It was the former longtime home of the founder of Yugoslavia, Marshal Josef Broz Tito. Milošević, who had reportedly been sleeping in a different bunker each night, was not home. But the attack sent an unmistakable message of personal peril and he eventually capitulated.

I don't know if my intervention was decisive. But I do know I spoke to President Clinton for forty minutes on Serbia and I do know that Milošević's home was bombed.

Milošević was finally forced from power—the subject of the later chapter "There Is No Substitute for Boots on the Ground"—and put on trial for genocide, crimes against humanity, and war crimes before an international tribunal in the Hague. He died of a heart attack before a verdict. I had used my access to the president, my proximity to the throne of power, to make my case. Some may say I was exploiting my position and exceeding my authority. All told, however, I feel vindicated.

JOE BIDEN

DEMETRIUS FREEMAN / THE WASHINGTON POST VIA GETTY IMAGES

Joe Biden won the presidency on his third attempt. Here the Democratic presidential nominee and his wife, Jill, join onstage with vice-presidential nominee Kamala Harris and her husband, Doug Emhoff, at the 2020 Democratic National Convention.

Truth 18

PREPARE FOR LUCK

You can never count on luck, but that does not mean you should not make yourself available in case fortune suddenly shines. Statistically, it may be unlikely that you will be lucky when you want to be. But over the course of a lifetime, you will inevitably get moments that favor you—so be ready.

JOE BIDEN SPENT his entire career waiting for the lightning of good fortune to strike. It struck twice.

At the age of twenty-nine, Biden was drafted in by local Democrats to fight what seemed sure to be a losing Senate race in Delaware against a popular longtime incumbent. Republican Cale Boggs, sixty-four, was a three-term congressman, a two-term governor, and a two-term senator, with 93 percent name recognition in Delaware. Biden, a public defender and county councilor, had name recognition of just 18 percent. One wag noted that Biden was younger than Senator Boggs's shoes. Polls showed him trailing 47 to 19 percent. "If I were a bookie, I'd give five-to-one odds right now that Boggs will be re-elected," Biden told the press.

Biden's national political career began as it would go on—with a gaffe. Before he formally entered the race, he referred to himself at an event as a "candidate"—only to row back later in the day to say he was only "90 percent sure." The *Wilmington News Journal* mocked him the next day with the headline, "Biden to (Oops) MAY Try Senate."

The 1972 election saw President Nixon crush his Democratic challenger, George McGovern, forty-nine states to one. Biden was one of the very few Democratic success stories that night. It was the first year that eighteen-year-olds could vote, and Biden's youth counted for him. "He understands what's happening today," his campaign ads proclaimed. Biden beat out Boggs by a meager 3,162 votes, or just over 1 percent.

"One wag noted that Biden was younger than Sen. Boggs's shoes."

Biden was so young that he only qualified to become a senator under the Constitution because he celebrated his thirtieth birthday thirteen days after the election—before he was actually sworn in. He told a reporter on election night: "I'm in a unique position. I'm thirty years old, the youngest senator down there. I might be able to sit there for another forty years if I'm a good boy and play my cards right."

As we saw in our earlier chapter "Suck It Up," Biden almost did not take up his seat because of the car-crash death of his wife and baby daughter, which left him as a single parent of their two infant sons. But once he got to the Senate, he stayed for thirty-six years—with eight more as presiding officer in his role as Obama's vice president.

Biden ran for president the first time in 1987, when he was just forty-four. His campaign imploded when he was accused of plagiarizing a speech by British Labour Party leader Neil Kinnock. He ran again in 2008, when he embarrassed himself by patronizingly complimenting rival candidate Barack Obama as "the first mainstream African-American who is articulate and bright and clean and a nice-looking guy." In neither presidential run did he exceed 1 percent of the primary vote.

At the 2008 Democratic National Convention, he opined: "Failure at some point in your life is inevitable, but giving up is unforgivable."

It was indeed third time lucky in 2020. America was not looking for a visionary statesman or a radical reformer. Amid the COVID-19 crisis, the country just wanted someone who did not recommend curing yourself by injecting bleach. Most Americans simply wanted someone, anybody, who was *not* Donald Trump. Biden stayed socially distanced in his basement and won nonetheless. He had what we describe in politics as "situational appeal."

Biden's 2020 victory completed his unlikely journey from youngest senator to oldest president. By the time he took the oath of office at age seventy-eight, he was older than the previous record-holder, Donald Trump, was when he left office at age seventy-four. He was even older than the record-holder before that, Ronald Reagan, was when he completed his *second* term at age seventy-seven.

For many years, Biden kept a framed cartoon on his desk. The first frame showed a man who was just struck by lightning shaking his fist at God and demanding: "Why me!?!" In the second panel, God responds: "Why not you?" For Biden, it serves as a reminder to accept his multiple misfortunes in life. But it is equally true for his stunning successes.

PART THREE

JUDGE YOUR TIMING

Time is the measure of all things. It is the greatest of all human inventions. Make good use of it.

BARACK OBAMA

President of the United States 2009–2017, US Senator 2005–2008

Barack Obama, a graduate of Harvard Law School '91, pictured here on campus, was told he couldn't rent a car when he went to the 2000 Democratic Convention. Eight years later, he was elected president.

Truth 19

TIME IS THE ONLY THING IN LIMITED SUPPLY

You can get more of everything—except time. Make sure you value it correctly, according to the laws of supply and demand. People like to say that "time is money," but in fact "money is time." Time is your most precious resource. And none of us know how much we have. So don't waste it. It is running out. Tick tock . . . tick tock . . .

IN 2000, A NOVICE politician in Chicago named Barack Obama suffered a thumping defeat by 31 points in his first run for Congress. To cheer him up, and restore his faith in politics, a friend invited him to that year's Democratic National Convention in Los Angeles.

Obama landed at LAX and went to the rental car counter. When he presented his American Express card, it was refused. The credit card—which he had used during his shoestring congressional campaign—was maxed out. Obama, just turned thirty-nine, a law professor and Illinois state senator, with one young daughter and another on the way, had to call the credit card company to plead to be allowed to take the car.

The little-known politico—who had enjoyed fifteen minutes of fame a decade earlier as the first Black president of the *Harvard Law Review*—arrived at the Staples Center to find that his friend had got him a pass that did not allow him onto the convention floor. So he had to watch the action on the TV screens outside. That evening, he was also refused entry to a convention party. He slept on the couch in his friend's hotel suite and flew back to Chicago early, while Al Gore was accepting the party's nomination. He considered giving up politics.

Four years later, Obama would deliver the keynote speech at the Democratic National Convention.

Eight years later, the convention would nominate him as the Democratic candidate for president.

Obama's victory in the 2008 election not only made him the first Black president of the United States but, at the age of 47 years and 169 days, the nation's fifth-youngest. And arguably its least experienced. From not being able to rent a car to winning the White House in the space of just eight years is one of the greatest accomplishments of American political history.

John F. Kennedy is the youngest US president so far, taking office in 1961 at the age of 43 years and 236 days. Like Obama, Kennedy was a US senator beforehand. But he was already in his second six-year term. Obama had only been in the Senate for four years. The only modern president with a shorter record in national politics than Obama was Dwight D. Eisenhower—and he was a sixty-two-year-old general and a transcendent national hero for winning World War II.

Despite the mocking of his wife, Michelle, Obama sensed the time was right.

"David Axelrod, Obama's own political adviser, had warned him that winning a Senate race in post–9/11 America was a reach for a Black man whose name rhymed with Osama."

The cards in the 2004 Senate race in Illinois broke his way. First, Carol Moseley-Braun, the first African-American woman senator, who had held the seat before, decided not to try to make a comeback bid. Then when Obama won the Democratic primary, his Republican opponent, Jack Ryan, a former Goldman Sachs investment banker, dropped out of the race in a sex scandal. Divorce papers revealed he had pressed his ex-wife, *Star Trek: Voyager* actress Jeri Ryan, to have sex with him in front of other people at sex clubs in New York, New Orleans, and Paris, including, she said, one "with cages, whips, and other apparatus hanging from the ceiling."

David Axelrod, Obama's own political adviser, had warned him that winning a Senate race in post-9/11 America was a reach for a Black man whose name rhymed with Osama. Axelrod suggested he wait to run for mayor of Chicago instead. But Obama's losing congressional race had convinced him that he could attract white support as well as Black. Ryan's replacement as the Republican candidate was the fire-breathing Christian Alan Keyes, who was also Black.

Obama's popularity in Illinois had made him a rising star of the Democratic Party. Just four years after he had difficulty renting a car, and could not get onto the convention floor, he was invited back to give the keynote address in Boston, with 9 million people watching on TV. Democrats wanted a signal to their African-American supporters, and at the same time to boost Obama's chances of picking up a Senate seat.

It is the genius of Obama that he perfectly read the craving of the nation for a healing unity after 9/11 and the divisive war in Iraq. He insisted there were not "Red States and Blue States" but just "one people." "There is not a Black America and a White America and Latino America and Asian America—there's the United States of America," he declared. After just seventeen minutes speaking, he was being compared to John F. Kennedy and Dr. Martin Luther King.

You can take all of us high-priced pollsters, strategists, and media consultants. We are all far less important than getting the message right and the timing right. If you get the message and the timing right, you win. It's as simple as that.

Obama won his race against Keyes by a record margin of 43 points to become the only African American in the Senate.

Almost as soon as he arrived, the press and even members of the public began asking Obama about whether he would run for president. Harry Reid, the Senate minority leader, summoned him to say that he thought he should stand in 2008. "Ten more years in the Senate won't make you a better president," Reid explained. Obama then consulted Edward Kennedy, the "Lion of the Senate," whose assassinated brothers John and Bobby had both run for president as senators and who had done so himself.

In his memoir *A Promised Land*, Obama records Ted Kennedy's sage advice: "I can tell you this Barack. The power to inspire is rare. Moments like this are rare. You think you may not be ready, that you'll do it at a more convenient time. But you don't choose the time. The time chooses you. Either you seize what may turn out to be the only chance you have, or you decide that you're willing to live with the knowledge that the chance has passed you by."

The conventional wisdom in politics that you need experience to run is actually wrong. You do far better in our system with no experience. Because if you run with experience you have a record you have to defend. Obama, having just become a senator, had virtually nothing to account for. On October 26, 2006, after less than two years as a Senator, Obama told Tim Russert on *Meet the Press* he was considering a run for president.

At the time, I was conducting polling for New York mayor Michael Bloomberg to test the waters for a potential independent run for president. My first reaction to Obama's entry into the race was, like Axelrod's to his Senate run, that it would be an uphill task. He faced Hillary Clinton in the Democratic primary and the "Clinton machine" built up over Bill's two presidencies. My polling in Iowa, the first primary state, showed, however, Hillary's serious weakness. I changed my view very quickly from "Obama can't win" to "Obama can't lose."

Obama's campaign brought out African Americans in record numbers and inspired the young in a way no one had since Bobby Kennedy and Eugene McCarthy in 1968. He managed to win the Left, inspired by his message of change, and the Center, with his calls to unity. He held white working-class voters much better than Hillary Clinton did in 2016 or Joe Biden did in 2020. Another decade in the Senate would have cost him dearly. In retrospect, it is clear to me that the 2008 election was the only presidential race Obama could have won. He saw that at the time—and the presidency was his deserved reward.

THE INSTITUTIONAL REVOLUTIONARY PARTY OF MEXICO

My client Vicente Fox celebrates becoming president of Mexico with a balloon caricature of himself given to him by a street child after he ended the record-breaking seventy-one-year rule of the country's Institutional Revolutionary Party.

Truth 20

INERTIA RULES

Possession is 90 percent of power. Those who are in want to stay in; those who are out want to get in. To get in, you have to oust those who are already in. Never underestimate the advantage of the incumbent.

MY ASSIGNMENT in Mexico in 2000 was simply to oust from power the world's longest-ruling political party.

The *Partido Revolucionario Institucional* (PRI), or Institutional Revolutionary Party, had run Mexico continually for seventy-one years since 1929. With the collapse of the Soviet Union, it had replaced the Soviet Communist Party as the party with the longest continuous grip on power. The novelist and failed Peruvian presidential candidate Maria Vargas Llosa once dubbed the PRI "the perfect dictatorship."

Its defeat in the election I had come to fight would be the Mexican version of the fall of the Berlin Wall.

The PRI had long exploited the benefits of incumbency, which we see all around the world, including the United States. Over the decades, the party had maintained its hold on power with a combination of ideological flexibility, patronage power, and outright fraud. Its leaders had ranged from President Lázaro Cárdenas, who nationalized the oil industry in the 1930s, to President Carlos Salinas de Gortari, who privatized state monopolies in the 1990s.

Successive presidents were picked by the outgoing leader, in a process known as the *dedazo*, or "finger." At election time, the party would truck voters to the polls and reward them with gifts. What it could not achieve legitimately, it achieved by cheating. The PRI won the 1988 presidential election only after the vote-counting computers mysteriously crashed when the opposition candidate was ahead. The 1994 campaign was upended by the as-yet-unsolved assassination of the original PRI candidate, Luis Donaldo Colosio, amid speculation he had been betrayed by his own party.

"The election I had come to fight would be the Mexican version of the fall of the Berlin Wall."

My candidate was a rancher and former Coca-Cola executive named Vicente Fox, representing the National Action Party (PAN). Standing 6'6" tall, and even taller in his favored cowboy boots, he towered over me and almost everyone else in Mexico. A conservative but fairly non-political businessman, Fox offered Mexico's turgid politics a pair of clean hands—and an end to PRI rule.

Fox was leading in all the opinion polls. But he was convinced that the PRI would steal the election once again unless they were stopped. He had seen what my firm had just done in Serbia—where our polling had stopped Slobodan Milošević from stealing victory—and wanted the same service in Mexico. The theory was that the involvement of a reputable American polling company, which had worked with President Bill Clinton, would guarantee that the result would be respected.

Our job, in short, was to stop the PRI from cheating again.

The PRI had tried to rebrand itself as the "New PRI." But the party was still up to many of its old tricks. PRI activists were handing out free chickens, tortillas, and T-shirts to voters and ferrying them to rallies in taxis. I was commissioned to conduct two pre-election polls, placing on record that Fox was ahead, and then to conduct exit-polling on election day itself.

It worked like a dream. It was the first presidential poll overseen by a new independent Election Commission. As soon as the results of the exit polls were clear, the Election Commission declared Fox the winner. To everyone's amazement, within three minutes the outgoing PRI president, Ernesto Zedillo, appeared on TV—even before the PRI presidential candidate, Francisco, could concede—to tell the public that Fox would be the next president. It seemed a message to his own party faithful: Do not try to cheat anymore.

It was a rare victory over the most entrenched incumbent—and Fox had wisely enlisted our help from north of the border to ensure it actually happened. Mexico's seventy-one-year era of one-party rule finally came to an end.

MICHAEL BLOOMBERG

People flee the collapse of the World Trade Center on September 11, 2001. Stephen Cooper, far left, later died from COVID-19.

Truth 21

THE WORLD CHANGES QUICKLY

Life does not move at an even pace. Many of the worst
events arrive by surprise. Be alive to respond to the new
circumstances. Sometimes that means literally staying
alive.

NO AMERICAN ELECTION has ever been disrupted as suddenly and violently as the New York primaries on September 11, 2001. Exactly two hours and forty-six minutes after the polls opened, the first hijacked airliner exploded into the North Tower of the World Trade Center, followed by the impacts at the South Tower, the Pentagon, and Shanksville, Pennsylvania. Almost 3,000 people died—including 2,753 innocent New Yorkers. It was one of those extremely rare one-day events that alter the course of history, on a par with the assassination of Archduke Ferdinand, Pearl Harbor, or Hiroshima. By the end of the day, the world was a completely different place. And particularly my hometown, New York City.

Michael Bloomberg, running for public office for the first time, rose early as he always does and walked from his five-story mansion on East Seventy-Ninth Street to the local polling station to see himself on the ballot as the Republican candidate for mayor. After casting his vote, he walked down to his campaign HQ on East Fifty-Sixth Street and started scanning the newspapers with a cup of coffee. Typically of Bloomberg, his desk was in a cubicle in the open-plan office. The TVs were on and someone alerted him that a plane had hit the World Trade Center. The TV anchor speculated that technical problems might have disrupted communications between air traffic control and the plane. "Bullshit!" Bloomberg, a licensed pilot himself, responded out loud, according to an account in *New York* magazine. "It's a crystal-clear day. These are visual-flying conditions. It has nothing to do with air-traffic control or any other mistakes."

"It was one of those extremely rare one-day events that alter the course of history, on a par with the assassination of Archduke Ferdinand, Pearl Harbor, or Hiroshima."

I also got up early and went to my polling station on Eighty-Eighth Street and Park Avenue. There, I ran into Bloomberg's beaming campaign manager, Patti Harris, handing out the campaign literature I had helped craft. She asked me to reassure her that Bloomberg would win the primary. Reassure her I did—but joked that she should remain at her post passing out campaign flyers to make absolutely sure.

I ate breakfast in a local coffee shop with my friend Mike Kramer, then a reporter for the *New York Daily News*. When we stepped out onto the sidewalk afterward, we both noticed that our cell phones had stopped working. We stepped into a phone store on Seventy-Third Street and Third Avenue to try to fix the problem. A moment later, a woman rushed into the store screaming: "They've hit the World Trade Center."

Neither of us immediately appreciated the full significance of the woman's cries. We hurried back to Kramer's apartment to check the news. I can still feel my utter shock when we turned on the TV and saw the Twin Towers spewing smoke into the downtown sky like Roman candles. Moments later, the unimaginable happened: The South Tower pancaked and collapsed in an enormous plume of dust. I had never witnessed such a macabre spectacle on such a monumental scale. To see the city I love, my city, maimed in this way remains one of the most painful moments of my life.

For months, I had been immersed in New York politics and the minutiae of the mayoral race. Suddenly, all that fell away. The primaries were halted mid-vote at 10:45. Like many New Yorkers, I sleepwalked through the next few days. Bloomberg was hit especially hard. Three of his employees had been attending a conference at the Windows on the World restaurant on the 106th floor of the North Tower, and he personally broke the news to the families. He refused to even talk about politics and insisted we stop polling until after the rescheduled primary.

There was never any doubt that Bloomberg would prevail in the Republican primary, as he did in the rescheduled vote on September 25. Our polling had consistently shown him trouncing Republican rival Herman Badillo, a local congressman. The outcome of the final mayoral race, pitting the novice Republican Bloomberg against the Democratic primary winner, Mark Green, looked, however, a great deal more difficult. New York is a Democratic bastion. As I had warned Bloomberg at the outset, the city had 3.6 million voters, of whom 2.4 million were Democrats. Bloomberg liked to joke later that not even his mother thought he could win.

It took a solid two weeks after 9/11 for the campaign to return to any degree of normalcy. My immediate reaction to the attacks was not even really anger,

but just an overwhelming lack of interest in anything, of disaffection, of ano-
mie. At the same time, I recognized that this unique set of circumstances—
which I hoped and believed would be a one-off attack—would set off a chain
reaction of consequences, both locally and around the world. Which of
course it did. That two-week pause gave us all valuable thinking time. The
world had changed suddenly and irrevocably, yes. But rather than act with
knee-jerk speed, we needed to take the measure of how the race had been
upended.

It became clear to me that in the changed post-9/11 world we needed a
new strategy in the mayoral race. The horrific crisis presented us with an
opportunity. The city needed leadership to get back on its feet. The public
craved an effective manager—exactly Bloomberg's greatest strength. I had
the hypothesis that New Yorkers needed a "revitalization plan." We tested it
in polling, and the voters agreed. We called it the "Five Boroughs Plan" and
started airing TV ads on it. We direct-mailed a copy of the plan to any New
York voters we thought we could win. Our polling showed that Bloomberg
had climbed to within single digits.

The other new factor was the incumbent Republican mayor, Rudolph
Giuliani. For some disconcerting minutes on 9/11, the loquacious Giuliani
had uncharacteristically disappeared from public view. When he reappeared,
striding dust-coated through Lower Manhattan after narrowly escaping the
collapse, Giuliani instantly metamorphosed from an unpopular lame-duck
incumbent who had recently undergone prostate cancer surgery and split
from his wife into a national hero acclaimed as "America's Mayor." *Time*
magazine would name him "Person of the Year 2001."

Giuliani's endorsement suddenly became pivotal for Bloomberg. When
Bloomberg had first gone to see him at the mayor's official residence at
Gracie Mansion before launching his bid, Giuliani had warned him: "You
are going to lose." In late October 2001, however, just two weeks before the
election, Giuliani agreed to publicly anoint Bloomberg as his successor.
Because he could not make a political endorsement from City Hall, we
redecorated a room at the Waldorf Astoria hotel to look like his mayoral
office. The result was a TV ad in which "America's Mayor" appeared to be
commanding his subjects to vote for Bloomberg.

Mark Green, the real estate scion who won the bitter Democratic primary, then made one of several blunders that would cost him the race. Green claimed he could have done as good a job as Giuliani, if not better. Playing on Green's reputation for arrogance, we turned his comments into an attack ad.

Giuliani's endorsement proved decisive right up to the final buzzer. On election day, early exit polling showed Bloomberg trailing by 2 percentage points. Bloomberg, on the verge of losing, convened a hasty conference call. When I began offering my rather verbose analysis, he cut me short and demanded to know: "What do we do about it?" We decided to pump out robo-calls to our potential supporters. Bloomberg recorded one message; Giuliani recorded another. Between 2:30 p.m. and the polls closing at 9:00 p.m., we made calls to almost three-quarters of a million people. It tipped the balance. Bloomberg won New York's post-9/11 mayoral election by 35,489 votes out of the total 1,480,582 cast. It was the slimmest margin of victory since George McClellan Jr., the son of the Civil War general, beat "yellow press" baron William Randolph Hearst in 1905. We had adapted skillfully but not precipitously to the changed world—and won.

SHIMON PERES

Then foreign minister Shimon Peres, left, with Prime Minister Yitzhak Rabin onstage at the "Yes to Peace" rally in Tel Aviv on Saturday, November 4, 1995—minutes before Rabin's assassination.

Truth 22

WHEN AVAILABLE, TAKE CERTAINTY...

When you see a window of opportunity, climb through it.

Don't wait. Certainty is a rare and precious thing in life.

When you are offered certainty, take it.

ON NOVEMBER 4, 1995, 100,000-plus Israelis thronged Tel Aviv's main square for a "Yes to Peace, No to Violence" rally to celebrate the Oslo Peace Accords. Side by side on the podium stood Prime Minister Yitzhak Rabin and his foreign minister, Shimon Peres, who had won the Nobel Peace Prize together with PLO chief Yasser Arafat for the Middle East peace deal. Beaming at the enormous crowd, Rabin told Peres, "This is beautiful." Despite their longstanding political rivalry, Rabin hugged him.

They had intended to leave the rally together, but their security team asked them to split up because of a credible threat to their lives. Peres walked down the steps of City Hall first to his car. As he bent down to climb in, he heard three shots. Yitzhak Rabin was dead—assassinated by a Jewish extremist.

At an impromptu late-night cabinet meeting, Peres, one of Israel's founding fathers, was named acting prime minister and acting defense minister of the shell-shocked nation. Israel had recently suffered a wave of Palestinian suicide bombings—four in 1994 and five in 1995—that had cost the Labor government support. But Rabin's assassination made him, in President Bill Clinton's words that very day, a "martyr for his nation's peace."

I had just started working for Rabin on the next Israeli election, due within a year. We finished our benchmark poll on Friday, November 3—the day before the assassination. Rabin had already signed off on our plan to distribute it that Monday. Rabin's murder was one of those moments when, as we saw in the previous chapter, the world changes very quickly. But my role in the forthcoming election remained the same. Although I had helped Menachem Begin defeat Peres fifteen years earlier, to his credit Peres bore no ill will. He asked me and my polling partner Zev Furst to stay on for the election.

"They had intended to leave the rally together, but their security team asked them to split up because of a credible threat to their lives."

We met Peres in the prime minister's office to present our first poll to him in early December 1995. He was unalterably convinced that he could not lose the next election. Many top Labor figures had urged him to call a snap poll to secure Rabin's legacy for another four years. But he rejected an early election out of hand. "To call an early election was to choose to win power using the spilled blood of Rabin," he later explained in his memoirs. "There was no reality, political or otherwise, in which I would use his death that way." Peres simply thought it would be ungentlemanly—as if there is anything at all gentlemanly about Israel's rough-and-tumble politics.

For Peres, the delay proved decisive. My life has taught me to take certainty over uncertainty. He simply refused to do so.

Furst and I tried to volunteer strategic initiatives that Peres could launch to win over key demographics like women voters and religious Jews. Although a personally charming man, he responded with barely concealed contempt. The only position for women in politics, he declared, "was prone." As for the religious Jews who could provide Peres with a winning margin, his answer was: "I will buy them when I need them because they are available for purchase."

Peres's opponent was Benjamin "Bibi" Netanyahu, the fast-talking former commando who had served as Israel's headline-grabbing ambassador at the United Nations. Netanyahu's right-wing Likud Party had been running a gloves-off campaign against Rabin. Before the assassination, Netanyahu had presided over two now-infamous rallies where there were chants of "Death to Rabin." Netanyahu had even rejected a request by Israel's internal security agency to dial down the rhetoric. Peres, betraying more than a little arrogance, stated his view to us very clearly: "I can't lose to a guy like that."

Polling showed Peres was up by 15 percentage points. But that was a fatal misreading of the polls. One in two voters knew who Peres was. Far fewer had heard much about the relative newcomer Netanyahu. You had to assume that everyone who was undecided would break for Netanyahu. When Peres did finally call the election, the telegenic Netanyahu demanded a TV debate. Peres, thinking himself comfortably ahead, flatly refused. I tried to talk him round, but he just would not listen.

Netanyahu was determined to hammer Peres for his dovish views. The suicide bombings continued with an attack on a public bus in Jerusalem and another at a Purim festival in Tel Aviv. Peres sought to blunt Netanyahu's security-focused campaign by getting me to ask another of my clients,

President Bill Clinton, to conclude a US–Israeli defense pact. Clinton was privately supporting Peres, but he flatly refused. He judged the move would complicate US relations with Arab nations. Netanyahu ran on the slogan "Netanyahu—Making a Safe Peace." I knew it would be effective. It was a variation of the same muscular slogan I myself had devised for Begin to beat Peres in 1981: "Peace Through Security."

I walked out of that first meeting with Peres believing that, despite his polling lead, he had as much chance of losing the election as of winning. This was the fifth time he had led Labor into an election. He had never won outright.

When the election finally took place on May 26, 1996—almost seven months after Rabin's killing—Peres lost by just 29,457 out of some 3 million votes cast. Netanyahu, forty-six, became Israel's youngest-ever prime minister and went on to become the longest-serving leader in Israeli history to date.

It proved to be Peres's last chance to become prime minister. A new four-year term would have offered him a historic opportunity to consolidate the Oslo Peace Accords that were so dear to him, and transform the Middle East. But he blew it. His timing was off.

BILL CLINTON

Bill Clinton, with Hillary watching on, tells the American people on January 26, 1998:
"I did not have sexual relations with that woman, Miss Lewinsky."

Truth 23

...OR STRATEGICALLY DELAY

There is always an urge to "do it yesterday." But that is by no means always the best approach. Often the circumstances call instead for delay, not action. Or call, indeed, for action to delay.

IT IS INDEED a sorry sight to watch the most powerful man in the world performing intellectual contortions to try to justify having an inappropriate relationship. It filled me with sadness.

Bill Clinton later confided to me that he knew he had no choice but to play for time when the Monica Lewinsky scandal broke with a leak to the *Drudge Report*. He correctly assessed that otherwise he would be unceremoniously booted out of the Oval Office. He explained he had to mischaracterize the relationship to save his presidency. Though the Lewinsky scandal was a tawdry, self-inflicted wound, his handling of it was a master-class in keeping hold of power. He understood the vital role of timing—and played it like the pro he was.

Clinton, re-elected to his second term, was first confronted with questions about Lewinsky under oath in the sexual harrassment case brought by Paula Jones. The former employee of the state-run Arkansas Industrial Development Corporation claimed that she had been summoned to Clinton's hotel room by a bodyguard during a conference hosted by the then-governor. And that Clinton had exposed himself to her. Jones's lawyers had been briefed about Clinton's Lewinsky liaison by Linda Tripp, the woman who befriended Lewinsky and persuaded her to keep her infamous semen-stained blue dress. The scandal broke on the *Drudge Report* on January 17, 1998—the very same day that Clinton was required to give a sworn deposition in the Paula Jones case.

Jones was receiving help from an anti-Clinton conservative legal foundation. But her legal team, knowing Clinton was a Yale Law grad and sometime law professor, tried to be too clever. To trap him in the deposition, Jones's lawyers drafted what they considered to be an exhaustive definition of what constituted "sexual relations" with Lewinsky. The definition stated that "a person engages in sexual relations when the person knowingly engages in or causes contact with the genitalia, anus, groin, breast, inner thigh, or buttocks of any person with an intent to arouse or gratify the sexual desire of any person." Clinton answered flatly: "I have never had sexual relations with Monica Lewinsky."

As Clinton insisted to me, the legal question was whether he had played any active role in his encounters with his twenty-two-year-old intern. It was a conversation between two lawyers, i.e., not a real-world conversation at all.

He insisted he had not had "sexual relations," because he had never touched any of the listed body parts with the intention of gratifying her, while she performed oral sex on him. It was a decidedly unchivalrous interpretation of what had gone on in the hallway off the Oval Office. According to him, Lewinsky had "sexual relations" with him, but he did not have "sexual relations" with her.

> **"It was a decidedly unchivalrous interpretation of what had gone on in the hallway off the Oval Office. According to him, Lewinsky had 'sexual relations' with him, but he did not have 'sexual relations' with her."**

This was the answer that eventually led to his impeachment. Clinton was asked repeatedly about the reported affair in the days that followed the *Drudge Report* story and denied it every time. On January 26, 1998, with wife Hillary standing at his side, he delivered his now infamous line to the American public: "I did not have sexual relations with that woman, Miss Lewinsky."

Later that year, Clinton was summoned to testify before a grand jury examining possible perjury in the Paula Jones case. Shortly before he did so, he called me on another matter and I took the opportunity to ask him why he would risk testifying to a grand jury. "I don't have a choice," he explained. "I got a Left-wing base in Congress. If I don't testify, they'll throw me out. That I know. They'll impeach me and I'll be gone."

Clinton understood timing on every level. In our private conversations, he told me later that year he had no choice but to deny the affair. "They would have hounded me out of office," he complained. His evasions, not to say outright lies, won him time to shore up his support. His timing—part of a delicate balancing act with Hillary, his party, and the electorate—enabled him to remain in power where Richard Nixon, who did not stay popular, could not.

MICHAEL BLOOMBERG

Michael Bloomberg, left, in the cramped office he dubbed "Starship Bloomberg" with the other founders of his company, Chuck Zegar, Tom Secunda, and Duncan MacMillan in 1982.

Truth 24

OUTWORK

It would be nice if we could all enjoy instant success, but aside from a few lucky Lotto winners that is impractical. Power is attained by steady, determined progress. Outworking other people gives you a sure, though incremental, advantage that over time yields enormous benefits. Think of it as getting a higher compound interest rate on your money, only this is compound interest on your labor.

MICHAEL BLOOMBERG has a favorite story he likes to tell, which is perhaps the most important story of his business career. After fifteen years of six-day weeks on Wall Street, he was fired by the investment bank Salomon Brothers in a restructuring at the age of thirty-nine. Rather than just "veg out" and enjoy his $10 million payoff, or go to work for someone else, Bloomberg resolved to become an entrepreneur.

He rented a 100-square-foot "broom closet" office on Madison Avenue with a view of an alley and set up his own firm. He recruited four former colleagues from Salomon Brothers—one of whom quit on the second day. Then he rented a second room next door and installed a coffee machine and a small refrigerator for sodas and went to work. The conditions were so poky that he once slammed the office door and found himself trapped inside when the lock broke.

Bloomberg's mission was to build a proprietary computer terminal that offered Wall Street traders real-time market data and financial analytics at the click of a key. It was the year the first IBM PC went on sale to the public, and Wall Street firms still stored their data on highly complex mainframes managed by teams of technicians. As recounted in his autobiography, *Bloomberg on Bloomberg,* he got a meeting at Merrill Lynch & Co to pitch his new product—which did not yet exist.

As was his custom, Bloomberg went into the negotiation alone. The Merrill Lynch team sitting around the forty-foot mahogany table included not just the head of the firm's Capital Markets Division, Ed Moriarty, who would make the final decision, but also a bevy of accountants, lawyers, salespeople, traders, and administrators as well as the company's in-house computer programmers. Bloomberg explained the potential of his planned black box. Moriarty turned to Merrill's software chief, Hank Alexander, and asked what he thought. Alexander suggested the firm simply do it themselves in-house. The firm's computer team, he said, could start work on it in six months.

Bloomberg seized his chance. "I'll get it done in six months and if you don't like it, you don't have to pay for it!" he vowed. Moriarty, seeing no downside, quickly assented and just got up and walked out of the room.

That left Bloomberg with the problem of delivering a still-nonexistent product to one of Wall Street's biggest firms in just six months. At the office they dubbed "Starship Bloomberg," fourteen-hour days became routine. Bloomberg remembers it as a "little electronics sweatshop." When they got too exhausted, the team would repair to a nearby movie theater. There was no quick fix. Bloomberg's team took the problem and broke it down into smaller manageable pieces. Over the days and weeks and months, they methodically addressed each component part with a camaraderie fueled by their common purpose. The final software fix was made as Bloomberg was riding in a taxi with his newly built terminal on the final day of the deadline to demonstrate it to Merrill Lynch.

"The final software fix was made as Bloomberg was riding in a taxi with his newly built terminal on the final day of the deadline to demonstrate it to Merrill Lynch."

Merrill purchased twenty-two of the new Bloomberg terminals. In time, they were followed by other Wall Street traders, the Bank of England, the Vatican, and the Federal Reserve. His initial $300,000 investment in the firm grew into a privately held company with more than 5,000 computer programmers and engineers and over 300,000 Bloomberg Terminals now valued at some $70 billion. As the company grew, Bloomberg continued to follow the same meticulous step-by-step approach.

He still does.

Though now eighty, Bloomberg still rises early to go to work. In my consulting work for him, I have frequently had meetings scheduled for 7:30 or 8:00 a.m. You are expected to be on time, because he is always punctual. When I was advising the garrulous President Clinton, meetings often turned into two-and-a-half-hour gab sessions. Not with Bloomberg. His meetings end at the scheduled time, if not before. Bloomberg does not tolerate long-winded discussion. He seeks practical solutions. When I first began consulting for him, I was told that I was lucky I got a chair in meetings. Many of his meetings are held standing up to stop people from wasting his time. As his autobiography concludes: "Work was, is, and always will be a very big part of my life."

When I was advising Italian prime minister Silvio Berlusconi, he once made a speech at a private dinner in his Roman villa extolling Bloomberg, then mayor of New York. Despite their very different personalities, the two billionaire businessmen and media moguls both have homes in Bermuda and are friends from there. Berlusconi lauded Bloomberg as an exceptional businessman, a great leader, and an extraordinary person. But he lamented that Bloomberg could not relax more. "I just wish he enjoyed life the way I do," he said.

When Bloomberg announced his run for president in 2019, one of the first people to call me was one of Berlusconi's closest aides. Berlusconi wanted to congratulate Bloomberg and offer his endorsement. I thanked him for his thoughts but decided that the public backing of the "bunga bunga"-loving Berlusconi would probably not help his chances.

MENACHEM BEGIN

Prime Minister of Israel 1977–1983

Although we were working closely together, Israeli prime minister Menachem Begin didn't tell me he was going to launch a daring raid on Saddam Hussein's Osirak nuclear reactor in Iraq just three weeks before Israel's 1981 election.

Truth 25

TAKE THE RISK

Try to measure your own propensity for risk-taking. You should certainly not seek risk, but neither should you be scared of it. When the odds are reasonable and the stakes are high enough, you should always be ready to act.

WITH JUST THREE weeks to go before Israel's 1981 election, I had absolutely no idea that my client was about to take dramatic and violent action that would totally upend the campaign, provoke international condemnation, and risk world peace.

He ordered a daring long-range bombing raid to destroy Iraq's Osirak nuclear reactor before Saddam Hussein could make nuclear weapons.

Menachem Begin, the prime minister, always seemed to me like an old-world gentleman. Three years earlier, he had struck the historic Camp David Accords with Egypt—Israel's first peace treaty with one of its Arab neighbors—and earned himself a Nobel Peace Prize. Beneath his formal manner, however, he was a man of steely resolve and unfaltering focus. In the wake of the Holocaust and the creation of Israel, he boasted of the rebirth of a "specimen completely unknown to the world for over eighteen hundred years, 'the FIGHTING JEW.'"

A Zionist hard-liner, he was once the most-wanted "terrorist" in British-run Mandatory Palestine. As head of the underground Jewish guerrilla group Irgun, he ordered the bombing of the British headquarters at Jerusalem's King David Hotel in 1946. The attack left ninety-one dead, including seventeen Jews, and made Begin a deeply polarizing figure in the newly created state of Israel.

For its first three decades, Israel had only Leftist governments—until Begin became the country's first right-wing prime minister in 1977. His stunning landslide is known in Israel as the *Mahapakh*, "upheaval," because it disrupted the prevailing order.

Despite Camp David, however, Begin's poll numbers had cratered by the time I joined him for the 1981 election. The economy had collapsed and inflation was running at 133 percent. Poll after poll showed his Labor Party opponent, Shimon Peres, with a double-digit lead. Begin responded by cutting taxes and allowing subsidies on luxury goods. That saw prices drop on everything from color TVs and stereos to beer and milk—and Begin's poll numbers began to recover.

Then came a bolt from the blue, literally.

On June 7, 1981, Begin authorized a squadron of eight heavily armed F16A jets with six F15A fighter escorts to launch a preemptive strike on the Osirak reactor outside Baghdad. To make the 2,000-mile round trip, the Israeli planes had to fly only a hundred feet above the desert to cross hostile Saudi Arabia. Israel's Mossad intelligence service had warned that the French-built reactor could start producing nuclear fuel within a month. Military planners had assumed that some pilots might be lost, but all returned safely to Etzion airbase with the mission accomplished. Saddam's reactor was destroyed.

"The raid was so audacious and unthinkable that the Israeli media at first did not believe it."

Coming just three weeks before a closely fought election, the raid was so audacious and unthinkable that the Israeli media at first did not believe it. When Begin's unfamiliar new spokesman called up the Israeli Broadcasting Authority, the editors feared it was a hoax. Only when Begin's journalist-nephew called his uncle to confirm the news did they believe it. Begin insisted Israel claim credit publicly as a deterrent for the future. But when the news finally broke, it came at 3:30 p.m. on the IBA's Radio Three pop music station.

Begin had risked Iraqi retaliation and international opprobrium. The United States was furious that Israel had kept the operation secret and joined the United Nations Security Council in condemnation. President Ronald Reagan wrote in his journal that day: "Got word of Israeli bombing of Iraq nuclear reactor. I swear I believe Armageddon is near." But Saddam Hussein, locked in his own war with Iran, stayed quiet.

I saw Begin in his office two days later to report that our polling showed an immediate bounce in his support. From a narrow lead of 3 or 4 points he had surged to 9 points in front. Some in Israel were complaining that he had timed the attack to gain electoral advantage. So I asked him directly.

Begin, frankly, looked exhausted—but calm, and confident of his world-shaking decision. "Look," he told me. "I didn't do this for political reasons. I know your government is going to condemn me, and the world is going to condemn me. But someday you will thank me for doing what I've done. I've kept Saddam Hussein from acquiring nuclear weapons for at least five to seven years. It was the right thing to do; it will preserve peace. Why would I do it three weeks before an election? If it was political, I wouldn't have done it in this way. But understand, it will take the world a long time to appreciate why I did what I did."

For Begin, the decision was all about "Never Again." His own mother and father and elder brother, and two four- and five-year-old cousins, were murdered in Poland during the Holocaust. Despite the protests of the opposition, I sensed zero political calculation. He explained that he had ordered the strike at the best time for Israel. The polls, he reflected, would probably rise in his favor for a while, but then fall back again. If he had wanted to use the Osirak raid to win, he would have timed it closer to the election.

Begin did eventually get the belated thank-you from the United States that he anticipated. A decade later, US defense secretary Donald Rumsfeld personally thanked the Osirak pilots "for making our job easier" in Operation Desert Storm to liberate Kuwait. The Osirak attack established the so-called "Begin Doctrine" that Israel would take preemptive action to stop Israel's enemies from acquiring weapons of mass destruction. In 2007, seven Israeli warplanes destroyed a suspected Syrian nuclear facility at Al-Kibar that was being built with North Korean assistance. The Begin Doctrine remains of supreme importance today as Israel seeks to prevent Iran from developing nuclear weapons.

As Begin put it to me: "Damn politics." The Osirak attack was a matter of life and death. He recognized the stakes and took the risk.

In the ensuing election, Begin's opponent, Shimon Peres, questioned the Osirak raid. He confirmed that he had been informed of the secret plan three months earlier but had expressed reservations. At my encouragement, Begin ran on a hawkish slogan of "Peace Through Security." It paid off. On June 30, Begin won a second term by half a percentage point.

PART FOUR

REWARD YOUR FRIENDS

Friendship is the foundation of power.

It can take the form of personal

relationships, or it can take the form of

political support. The magic moment is

when a leader finds their followers. But

that bond must be nurtured too.

■

"THE WEST SIDE KIDS"

I learned my trade as part of the "West Side Kids" on New York's Upper West Side, scene of the classic 1961 film West Side Story.

Truth 26

YOU ARE YOUR FRIENDS

No man, as the poet said, is an island. We are all shaped and defined by our friends—for good or bad. The rest of the world sees us in our context. So be thoughtful about whom you frequent.

MY FIRST EXPERIENCE of political campaigning—the activity I would devote my life to—came on the D Train subway line to Coney Island in 1969. Robert A. Low, the Democratic councilman for New York's "Silk Stocking" district and a family friend at our synagogue on the Upper East Side, was running for City Council president. Still a sixteen-year-old junior at the Horace Mann prep school, I was enlisted to plaster "Bob Low for City Council President" posters at subway stations. For this illegal vandalism, I was promised $25. When I stepped off the train at Coney Island, a cop was waiting. He told me the fine was $50—but let me go.

It was the old-style scattershot approach to campaigning. Bob Low lost.

Shortly afterward, I met a friend-of-a-friend called Jerrold "Jerry" Nadler, a recent Columbia University graduate who was the newly elected Democratic district leader for New York's Upper West Side. Nadler, himself just twenty-one, said that power in the area was passing to a new group led by a secretive political genius named Dick Morris. "He will be one of the top strategists in America very soon—if he isn't already," he vowed. I was flattered that Morris wanted to meet me.

When I arrived at Morris's shabby apartment building on Riverside Drive at Ninety-Fifth Street, I was surprised to be welcomed by a baby-faced twenty-two-year-old in a button-down shirt holding a glass of orange juice. His then-wife, Gita, presented us with some take-out chicken and we sat down to talk politics. "I know things about political organizing that no one else does," Morris boasted. "Sign on, and you'll learn them too." The introduction changed my life.

I had joined the "West Side Kids."

Morris and his young acolytes planned to take control of the Democrat-dominated Upper West Side and use it as a power base to take over New York. Like Nadler, Morris had gone to Stuyvesant High School, the high-powered New York public school then on East Fifteenth Street. In fact, Morris had run Nadler's successful campaign to become class president. I enlisted in their effort to elect another Stuyvesant alum, Dick Gottfried, Morris's old high-school debating partner, to the New York State Assembly.

It was a revelation to me. Morris had gone through the voter list on an apartment building–by–apartment building basis. He could tell you who the

leaders were in each building, what they thought, and what issues mattered
to its residents. This type of micro-targeting is now routine in politics—but
back then it was revolutionary. When we called our likely voters, we delivered
tailored messages. Morris dispatched hand-picked canvassers to each building. He refused, for instance, to send me into the large apartment complex
called Lincoln Towers because he said it was controlled by activists from Al
Shanker's United Federation of Teachers. He felt that I, as a sixteen-year-
old, was ill-equipped to argue with veteran Leftists. Instead, I was deployed
among what he called the "undifferentiated Leftists" who inhabited the then
largely rent-controlled buildings along Central Park West, now one of the
most expensive streets in America.

Morris and the "West Side Kids" were a nerdy offshoot of the anti–
Vietnam War movement who decided to work for change within the system, not outside it. While other young people were protesting in the streets,
Morris, Nadler, and Gottfried struck a down-and-dirty deal for support with
James R. McManus, the district leader whose Irish clan had long dominated
the Democratic Party in the Hell's Kitchen area of Midtown Manhattan. It
was an act of pure *Realpolitik*.

**"'I know things about political organizing
that no one else does,' Dick Morris boasted.
'Sign on, and you'll learn them too.'
The introduction changed my life."**

Gottfried won his 1970 campaign—and remained in the State Assembly
for fifty-two years until announcing his retirement in 2021. He is the longest-
serving legislator in New York's history. Nadler became a state assemblyman
and then a congressman. He has been in the House of Representatives since
1992.

Morris tried to convince me to abandon my plans to go to Harvard to
attend Columbia University instead and remain active with the "West Side
Kids." He said he could guarantee I would be a district leader within two
years, the first step on the ladder for an elected official. But I was not ready

to sacrifice my academic future, regular friendships, girls, and all the other fruits of youth, to pursue his program of full-immersion politics.

Though I turned down his offer, and did indeed leave New York to go to Harvard, I can now appreciate how much I learned as a "West Side Kid." Their innovative techniques of exhaustive canvassing to build a comprehensive database of voters, the segmenting of the electorate, the use of tailored messaging, the targeted effort to turn out favorable voters, and even the *Realpolitik* of the McManus deal have all shaped my approach to electioneering ever since.

Morris did indeed go on to become one of America's preeminent political consultants—until a scandal over a call girl who claimed not only that he liked sucking her toes but that he showed her drafts of President Clinton's speeches and allowed her to listen in on a private call with him. After working on the Upper West Side, I lost touch with Morris for twenty years until I happened to rent a house near him in Redding, Connecticut. When we reestablished contact, he engineered my entry into the White House to work for Clinton—the first time I had worked for a US president.

I realized even at the time that my scattershot campaigning for Bob Low on the subways was the past. I also understood that the new-style campaigning of Morris, Nadler, and Gottfried and the "West Side Kids" was something I could learn from—and I did. That two-year period taught me more about political campaigning than any other experience in my life. I don't mind admitting that my political consultancy and polling business monetized many of the ideas I learned from the "West Side Kids."

LOBBYING

David Bossie, the president of the conservative non-profit Citizens United, stands in front of a poster for Hillary: The Movie, *which triggered the landmark 2010 Supreme Court ruling allowing unlimited campaign spending by corporations and billionaires.*

Truth 27

YOU CAN EARN YOURSELF A LOT OF GOODWILL VERY CHEAPLY...

Gestures of goodwill are too rare and therefore much appreciated. They can often yield a disproportionate result. Volunteer goodwill and you will receive goodwill back. Some call it "karma," others just a "return on investment."

IF YOU WENT to Washington and let it be known that you had a quarter of a million dollars burning a hole in your pocket and you wanted to see the Speaker of the House to discuss your pet issue, you would likely get an invitation to meet him or her within a few days. You might even get in to see the vice president.

If you went to Harvard and said you had the same amount to donate and wanted to meet the university president to discuss your child's application, you wouldn't get in the door. The Harvard president, to paraphrase super-model Linda Evangelista, doesn't get out of bed for a quarter of a million dollars. That will cost you a seven- or eight-figure sum.

The stark truth is that in America today, it is cheaper to purchase a meeting with the most powerful people in the Free World—the second and third in line to the presidency—than it is to get time with a college president in Massachusetts.

It is surprisingly cheap in life, as it is in politics, to buy yourself valuable—and lucrative—goodwill.

There are, I can assure you, great bargains to be had in American politics. Politicians have a voracious need for campaign contributions and are ready to repay the favor with favorable tweaks to legislation. While your cash goes into their own campaign coffers, their repayment comes not from their own pocket but from taxpayer money. Often they are giving what they would have given anyway. Or simply stopping something you don't want—like a tax rise—from happening.

It is an open secret in Washington that legislators do not actually read the voluminous legislation they enact, leaving that tiresome task to aides and lobbyists. And the president has no line-item veto to remove the pork. So the back-room deals are buried in the fine print and are all but invisible to the voters.

When I started my career as a political consultant, lobbying was a sleepy profession concentrated on Washington's "K Street," where old-style influence-peddling took place over three-Martini lunches in fancy restaurants. It harked back to the British origin of the word in the practice of hanging round the lobby outside Parliament. Now, however, lobbying is a highly professionalized, hi-tech business populated by former congressmen, ex-senators, and top government officials who have gone through the "revolving door."

The explosive growth of lobbying is changing the nature of our democracy. We set up our system based on the "consent of the governed." We are moving to a corporate democracy based on the "consent of the super-PAC." Increasingly, the voter matters little. Elections are becoming a contest between competing corporate interests who fund candidates, hire lobbyists, and mobilize grassroots campaigns to represent them. It is now possible for a group of lobbyists to get together and literally pick and fund a candidate for a local, state, or congressional race.

"There are, I can assure you, great bargains to be had in American politics. Politicians have a voracious need for campaigning contributions and are ready to repay the favor with favorable tweaks to legislation. While your cash goes into their own campaign coffers, their repayment comes not from their own pocket but from taxpayer money."

The 2010 Supreme Court ruling in *Citizens United vs. Federal Elections Commission* barely registers in the public consciousness—but it changed the world. It deserves to be an election issue. It needs to be reversed to save our democracy.

The conservative non-profit Citizens United was founded as a political action committee (PAC) in 1988 by Floyd Brown, the son of a sawmill worker turned political consultant. Brown earned notoriety by producing the infamous "Willie Horton" ad in the 1988 presidential campaign blaming Democratic candidate Michael Dukakis for releasing a Black murderer from jail on a "weekend pass" furlough to allow him to rob and rape again. It was widely condemned for its nasty racial undertones — but it helped George H. W. Bush win the White House.

In 2008, Citizens United produced an anti–Hillary Clinton documentary to oppose her run for the Democratic presidential nomination. The 2002 Bipartisan Campaign Reform Act, also known as "McCain-Feingold," barred corporations and non-profits from making any "electioneering communications" close to a vote. Citizens United challenged the law all the way up to America's highest court.

The Supreme Court ruled that the First Amendment protection of free speech guaranteed the right of corporations and non-profits to make independent expenditures for political campaigns. The 5–4 ruling opened the floodgates for corporations and wealthy individuals, acting through super-PACs, to spend unlimited amounts to back their favored candidates. The court essentially ruled that corporations have the same free speech rights as private individuals.

It's an alarming idea, since corporations are so much richer and more powerful than most citizens. Justice John Paul Stevens warned in his dissent: "When citizens turn on their televisions and radios before an election and hear only corporate electioneering, they may lose faith in their capacity, as citizens, to influence public policy. A government captured by corporate interests, they may come to believe, will be neither responsive to their needs nor willing to give their views a fair hearing. The predictable result is cynicism and disenchantment."

A follow-on case from *Citizens United*, called *SpeechNow vs. FEC*, allowed individuals to band together to form super-PACs for political campaigns, using these organizations to escape limits on individual campaign contributions. super-PACS can now be formed under section 501(c)c of the Internal Revenue Code, which requires disclosure of donors, or section 501(c)4, which does not. The latter is so-called "dark money."

The *New York Times* has calculated that anonymous donors spent at least $2.4 billion of "dark money" on the 2020 presidential election (at least $1.5 billion for Democrats and $900 million for Republicans). This "dark money" exceeded even the record total raised by the candidates themselves ($1 billion by Joe Biden and $810 million by Donald Trump).

Precisely because you can buy yourself a lot of goodwill very cheaply, the *Citizens United* ruling poses a danger to our system of "government of the people, by the people, for the people" described by Abraham Lincoln in the Gettysburg Address. The Supreme Court has empowered corporate interests in a way that may not be corrupt per se but which corrupts the system. Corporations and billionaires don't just come in with bags of cash and buy influence. But the power differential has shifted so heavily to those with super-PACs that the nature of our society has changed profoundly.

BENJAMIN (BIBI) NETANYAHU

Prime Minister of Israel 2009–2021, 1996–1999

ABIR SULTAN, POOL VIA AP

Benjamin Netanyahu and Naftali Bennett, seen here in the Israeli cabinet in 2016, were once friends and allies but fell out over, among other things, Netanyahu attacking Bennett's "non-kosher" pastry chef wife.

Truth 28

...AND YOU CAN EARN YOURSELF A LOT OF BAD WILL EVEN CHEAPER

Delivering a personal slight might be momentarily satisfying and give you a fleeting sensation of power. But it is never worth the long-term cost. Scrupulously avoid giving slight injury. If you are going to hurt someone, make sure you cripple them. Otherwise you leave them the opportunity for revenge.

IN LATE 2014, Bibi Netanyahu, the prime minister, invited me to Israel. I had worked against Netanyahu in the country's 1996 election, but—as we saw in the chapter on "When Available, Take Certainty"—my candidate, Shimon Peres, delayed and suffered an upset defeat that allowed Netanyahu to become prime minister for the first time. So no hard feelings there obviously. Netanyahu is a man of politics, through and through, and would go on to become his country's longest-serving leader. He told me he had watched me on TV and had great respect for my expertise. I was, frankly, flattered he sought my advice.

Netanyahu and I spent five hours in conversation about Israeli politics and particularly about Israel's relations with its all-important ally, the United States. Netanyahu had clashed repeatedly with President Obama over his attempts to negotiate a nuclear deal with Iran. Never could he have imagined, he complained, that he would be closer to Egyptian president Abdel Fattah el-Sisi or Saudi Crown Prince Mohammed bin Salman than he was to the American president. He wanted my take on how he should deal with the United States.

My professional advice was that Israel and Netanyahu himself should go over the head of President Obama to the US Congress and the American people. For fully an hour and a half we discussed how Israel needed a public strategy in the United States that involved approaching sympathetic legislators directly. He thanked me for my recommendations—and told me I was hired.

I never heard from him again.

In my business, it is easy for a leader to get an aide to pick up the phone and say, "Thank you for your time." He didn't even do that.

"Small insults add up. Avoid them. They are never worth the cost. If you are going to insult someone, at least get your money's worth."

Not long afterward, Netanyahu addressed a rare joint session of Congress. The Republican House Speaker, John Boehner, and Senate Majority Leader Mitch McConnell invited him without consulting the Obama administration in advance. Obama's vice president Joe Biden, who would normally sit behind him on the dais, refused to attend. Netanyahu undiplomatically lectured Congress and the American public that Obama's Iran nuclear deal was a "bad deal." His forty-minute speech was interrupted by applause twenty-nine times. I can assure you, no one sent me a ticket.

While it might have been understandable that Netanyahu would not invite me to the centerpiece of his US outreach, what was not acceptable was that he never paid my bill. He did not even reimburse my airfare as promised. I had never been shortchanged by a world leader like that before. What surprised me more than anything was that when I mentioned it to other Israelis, they just shrugged. "That is Bibi," they explained. "He does that to everyone."

Small insults add up. Avoid them. They are never worth the cost. If you are going to insult someone, at least get your money's worth.

Netanyahu is one of the most slippery politicians I have ever had the dubious honor to deal with. So it did not surprise me when he was eventually indicted for bribery, fraud, and breach of trust. The prosecution centered on allegations that he had traded favors for positive media coverage in Israel. Some of the claims reveal his pettiness. At one point, for instance, Netanyahu allegedly targeted the wife of his own former chief of staff, Naftali Bennett, who had broken with Netanyahu to found his own right-wing movement. Israel's Channel 12 television reported that Netanyahu personally asked the owner of the Walla news website to publish a report that Bennett's wife, Gilat, a professional pastry chef who once worked at New York's Aureole, Amuse, and Bouley Bakery, now baked at non-kosher restaurants in Israel. The slight would cost Netanyahu dearly. If there is one thing worse than insulting a man, it is surely insulting his wife. Naftali Bennett responded on Twitter: "I feel sorry for you, Mr. Netanyahu."

Netanyahu's 2019 indictment paralyzed Israeli politics through four snap elections that were effectively a four-episode psychodrama about Netanyahu. He was eventually deposed in 2021. What finally unseated him was a motley coalition of eight parties, ranging from Islamist Israeli-Arabs to Leftists to right-wing Jewish religious parties, whose sole point in common was that they wanted to dump Netanyahu out of office.

Tellingly, the anti-Netanyahu coalition that took power included three parties headed by disaffected former allies. Gideon Sa'ar of the New Hope party was once Netanyahu's No. 2 in the Likud party. Avigdor Lieberman of Israel Our Home and Bennett of Yamina had both served as Netanyahu's chief of staff. The new administration was an all-star team of Netanyahu's erstwhile aides: Sa'ar became the minister of justice and deputy prime minister; Lieberman became the finance minister; and Bennett—the one with the pastry chef wife—became the new prime minister.

Almost immediately following his ouster, remaining members of Netanyahu's Likud began grousing in the pro-Netanyahu mass circulation *Israel Hayom* newspaper that he had alienated his own team. Netanyahu was "suddenly trying to go back to basic human relations, the lack of which got him into the trouble he's dealing with today," one unnamed former Likud minister complained. "Suddenly he's trying to be nice" but "no one believes him."

LINDA TRIPP

Pentagon staffer 1994–2001, White House staffer, 1991–1994

Linda Tripp was a nobody in Washington—until she revealed President Clinton's relationship with Monica Lewinsky.

Truth 29

EVERYONE CAN HELP YOU AND EVERYONE CAN HURT YOU

Pay attention to everyone in your peripheral vision. Help can come from unexpected quarters—and so can harm.

IN THE YEARS I worked in the White House, throughout the entire Monica Lewinsky affair, I never once heard President Clinton utter the name Linda Tripp.

I'd be surprised if the Leader of the Free World had more than a vague idea who she was, a faceless civil servant floating around the West Wing—until it was too late.

Tripp was a completely insignificant figure in Washington—until she wasn't.

The daughter of a US Army sergeant she described as a "raging bully," Tripp married an Army first lieutenant, becoming an "officer's wife." She followed her husband to Europe, where she worked with a top secret security clearance as an assistant to a US military representative to NATO. The pair then returned to the United States where she joined the secretive support staff of the Delta Force at Fort Bragg, North Carolina. When she got divorced, a single mother of two kids, she transferred to the Pentagon. But it was her next move that set her on the path to notoriety.

In April 1991, Tripp was hired to the Correspondence Unit of the White House of President George H. W. Bush. The team, which handled the president's mailbag of 18 million letters a year, was housed in the Old Executive Office Building overlooking the White House. But Tripp herself was assigned to be a "floater" who provided support where needed. She soon found herself "floating" in the West Wing of the White House, working for the chief of staff just steps from the Oval Office. She got the title executive assistant to the deputy chief of staff to the president.

> **"Tripp admits that her troubled relationship with her own father made her intolerant of Clinton's misbehavior, calling the president 'the supreme bully.'"**

Since she had risen in the Bush White House, Tripp fully expected when President Clinton was elected that she would be sent back to the Old Executive Office Building. Instead, she got a call on vacation after the inauguration asking her to report to the Immediate Office of the President, the Oval Office staff. When she suggested sending another "floater," she was told the incoming Clinton administration had requested her by name. Big mistake.

The call put her in the immediate proximity to power—and soured her on the Clintons, plural. In her posthumous memoir, A Basket of Deplorables, she describes the clash more as one of ethics and values than of politics. She objected to Clinton's staff turning up for work in sweatshirts, jeans, and sneakers and to Hillary's open swearing. "The counterculture had taken over . . ." she wrote. "It was as if the radicals of the Sixties had finally taken over the school and thrown out everything in their way."

Tripp was particularly offended when Hillary fired her former colleagues in the Correspondence Unit—which still paid her salary—to replace them with Clinton loyalists. She grew more upset when the same fate hit the professionals at the White House Travel Office, amid suspicion the Clintons wanted to channel the business to a donor. Even the White House barber was replaced. Tripp admits that her troubled relationship with her own father made her intolerant of Clinton's misbehavior, calling the President "the supreme bully." But it is striking in her memoir how it was Hillary who really inspired her anger. "As bad as he was, Hillary was a lot worse," Tripp writes.

Tripp found herself in the anomalous position of being virtually the only professional non-political civil servant in a West Wing staffed by Clinton loyalists. She was one of the first people to see donor Kathleen Willey, breathless and disheveled, and touching up her lipstick, emerging from the Oval Office after what Willey later claimed was a sexual assault by Clinton. After the suicide of adviser Vince Foster, Tripp was the person who phoned for a uniformed Secret Service guard when she saw Clinton staff "straightening out" his office.

As she long anticipated, Tripp was shipped out of the West Wing herself and transferred in the summer of 1994 to the Public Affairs Office at the Pentagon—with a juicy 45 percent pay raise. The Clinton White House could be forgiven for thinking it had neutralized any threat her disloyalty posed.

Two years later, however, the Clintons sought to solve another problem by exiling another person from the White House to the very same Public

Affairs Office at the Pentagon: Lewinsky herself. Another big mistake. Tripp's explanation is that Ken Bacon, the assistant secretary of defense for public affairs, was an "uber-loyalist" who would unquestionably accept any staff the White House sent over. The besotted Lewinsky could not resist confiding in Tripp, a fellow White House refugee, about her Oval Office trysts with Clinton. Seeing the opportunity to expose Clinton's behavior, and get even, Tripp began secretly recording their conversations.

It was these twenty hours of recordings that Tripp passed to Special Prosecutor Ken Starr to show Clinton had lied about his relationship with Lewinsky. The evidence, and Lewinsky's revelation to Tripp that she kept a semen-stained blue dress from one encounter with the president, led to Clinton's impeachment—although he was acquitted by the Senate—and forever tarnished his reputation.

It is worth underlining that Tripp did not even know Lewinsky until the two met at the Pentagon, where they had both been exiled by the Clinton White House.

Tripp justified her duplicity by insisting she was protecting a "narcissistic" child from a "sexual predator." Lewinsky, who always intended to cover up for Clinton, said simply: "I hate Linda Tripp." The recent TV series *American Crime Story: Impeachment* cast Tripp as the super-villain with actress Sarah Paulson wearing a padded suit to parody her bulky frame. But the show updated Tripp's image for the "Me-Too" era. As the *New Yorker* said of her portrayal in the show: "Tripp is abusive and conniving. But she is also a person—one who happened to be right about Clinton." It is an intriguing conclusion given that one of its producers, who played a central role in publicizing the series, is the now-middle-aged Monica Lewinsky.

TED CRUZ

US Senator 2013–

Senator Ted Cruz, third from left, seen here with fellow Republican presidential candidates Ben Carson, Donald Trump, and Jeb Bush in 2015, eventually had to make nice with Trump even though Trump called him "Lyin' Ted" and suggested his father was involved in the assassination of President Kennedy.

Truth 30

YOU HAVE TO
GIVE TO GET

It is nice to fantasize about absolute power, but the truth is that power is a two-way street. You cannot just take; but you must not just give. That is the core of politics and life: compromise—even when it is excruciatingly painful.

IN THEIR BITTER Republican primary of 2016, Donald Trump branded him "Lyin' Ted." He suggested Ted Cruz's Cuban-born father may have aided and abetted Lee Harvey Oswald in assassinating President Kennedy. He questioned Cruz's evangelical faith, observing that "not too many evangelicals come out of Cuba, okay." Hardest to take was Trump tweeting an unflattering photo of Cruz's wife implying she was ugly.

Cruz, a senator from Texas, denounced Trump as a "sniveling coward," a "pathological liar," a "serial philanderer," a "big loud New York bully," and "a narcissist at a level I don't think this country's ever seen." Warning of his "Trumpertantrums," he predicted: "We're liable to wake up one morning and Donald, if he were president, would have nuked Denmark." When Trump beat him for the nomination, Cruz told the Republican convention he refused to endorse him because he didn't support people "who attack my wife and attack my father."

History records that Cruz did endorse Trump soon afterward (and that Trump did not nuke Denmark). Shortly after Trump became president, Cruz took his wife and two young daughters to dinner with him at the White House, describing his host as "warm and gracious." The following year, *Time* magazine asked Cruz to pen the encomium to Trump for its list of the 100 Most Influential People. "President Trump is a flash-bang grenade thrown into Washington by the forgotten men and women of America," he wrote fawningly.

Cruz and I had the same professor at Harvard Law School. Alan Dershowitz tells me that Cruz was one of the two smartest students he ever had. (He also admitted that I was not the other one—although he kindly suggested I was probably the wisest.) Before going into politics, Cruz clerked for Chief Justice William Rehnquist and later, as Texas solicitor general, argued nine cases before the Supreme Court.

Cruz can sometimes look ridiculous and seem humiliated. But he is by no means a stupid guy. So what is he up to?

He is following one of the cardinal rules of politics: You have to compromise with power. If there is something you want, you will invariably have to give something in return. Cruz no doubt still dreams of becoming president, although Trump still stands in his way. He may also hope to snag a Supreme Court nomination from a future Trump administration. These are big asks and require a major political quid pro quo.

Trump hit the nail on the head when he said, the day after Cruz's speech at the 2016 Republican convention, that Cruz may have ruined his political career. Despite widespread ridicule, Cruz took the necessary steps to save it.

"Ted Cruz and I had the same professor at Harvard Law School. Alan Dershowitz tells me that Cruz was one of the two smartest students he ever had."

Cruz, who won election in 2012 as a Tea Party–backed insurgent, has a knack for political stunts. He once made a twenty-one-hour speech reading *Green Eggs and Ham* by Dr. Seuss on the Senate floor in an unsuccessful bid to filibuster funding for Obamacare. But his self-interested politicking has provoked the ire of his Republican colleagues. Fellow senator Lindsey Graham once joked: "If you killed Ted Cruz on the floor of the Senate, and the trial was in the Senate, nobody would convict you."

Politics is about dealing with reality, not the world as you wish it would be. The reality of political power is that Cruz had little choice but to accommodate himself to Trump.

Senator Graham delivered this home-truth when he said on *Fox News Sunday*: "Donald Trump is the most consequential Republican in the entire Republican Party, maybe in the history of the party since Ronald Reagan. And if you're going to lead this party in the House and the Senate, you have to have a working relationship with Donald Trump or it will not work."

Cruz has been willing to offer up his entire political identity on the altar of Donald Trump. But the sacrifice was more than worthwhile: It was essential. When Trump's influence looked to be waning in the aftermath of the January 6 assault on Congress, Cruz tried to distance himself by describing it as a "violent terrorist attack on the Capitol." But Trump did not fade and Cruz was soon back on-air on Fox News trying to appease him. In an excruciating interview with Tucker Carlson, Cruz apologized and called his own comments "frankly dumb."

It was another purely power-politics calculation by one of the smartest students ever to graduate from Harvard Law.

DONALD TRUMP

Donald Trump, running for president, talks to adoring fans at a campaign rally in Phoenix, Arizona, on July 11, 2015. The New York Times *called his speech a "rambling monologue."*

Truth 31

FIND YOUR FOLLOWERS

You can make friends of people you don't even know. If you can express what they themselves desire, they will identify with you. And in some cases even idolize you.

THE FIRST TIME I realized that Donald Trump had a political future was when I saw him at his casinos in Atlantic City. The casinos were heading for bankruptcy. Yet when he arrived, people would rush toward him to shake his hand or just to touch him, as they would a religious figure.

This frenzied reaction was a function of the fame he had achieved for his gold-plated lifestyle in the New York gossip columns. It was the type of publicity that meant regular Joes saw a connection to him as aspirational. Even in his own casinos, where the house never loses, punters treated him as a talisman of good luck.

The market research I performed for him revealed a similar phenomenon. Trump had already plastered his name over his buildings, particularly the lavish Trump Tower, his casinos, and his Trump Shuttle airline. When we studied the surveys, however, we found that nothing about the casinos themselves or the entertainment or the restaurants or the planes explained their attraction. Their unique selling proposition was Trump himself. That said to me that he had—and indeed has—a unique appeal.

At the launch of his 2016 presidential campaign, Ivanka Trump praised her father's record across a variety of industries, which is dubious to say the least. But she was correct when she said: "The common denominator is him! His vision, his brilliance, his passion, his work ethic, and his refusal to take 'no' for an answer." Whatever industry he is in, he is basically in the business of branding it with his name. His greatest business innovation was that you could brand buildings the way you can brand handbags or sneakers.

When I conducted Trump's first private presidential poll in 1987, he was planning to run as a moderate independent, not the hard-right Republican he is today. He was once a registered Democrat. For a time, he was even pro-choice. Yet he had already identified—if not specifically proclaimed— his populist message. His first full-page newspaper ads in 1987 picked up on popular discontent about the US Navy protecting Japanese oil tankers in the Persian Gulf—for free. "End our huge deficits, reduce our taxes, and let our economy grow unencumbered by the cost of defending those who can easily afford to pay us for the defense of their freedom." This nativist salvo foreshadowed by twenty-nine years his winning "America First" message of 2016.

Trump has an uncanny ability to pick up the messages that voters are most responsive to—and to run with them. He's prepared to play whatever role he needs to play. It's all role-playing with him. As his former lawyer-turned-nemesis Michael Cohen writes in his book *Disloyal*: "Doing anything—and I mean anything—to 'win' has always been his business model and way of life."

"Even in his own casinos, where the house never loses, punters treated him as a talisman of good luck."

The media loves to catch Trump in his lies. The *Washington Post's* Fact Checker column, started in response to Trump, found that he had spoken 30,573 untruths in the four years of his presidency—averaging about twenty-one falsehoods a day. Add to that the "Big Lie" he has told since leaving office denying President Biden's victory in the 2020 election. But the media's game of "gotcha" misses the essential point: He simply does not care.

From my private conversations with Trump, I can say he has a very good and accurate memory. Like all of us he is fallible, but he is not somebody who lives in a world of delusion. But he does live in a world of illusion . . . that he creates. Trump thinks his lying helps him. He knows perfectly well what he is doing. The underlying message is: "I will stand up and say what is on my mind (even if you won't)."

Like former Italian leader Silvio Berlusconi, Trump has an entertainer's instinct to follow his audience. Hence his rambling and unpredictable speeches, so often ridiculed in the media but fascinating to those in attendance. Even when he is addressing a crowd of 50,000 or 100,000 people, he makes each person feel it is a one-on-one event. You feel you are getting insights that are otherwise not available to you. As a seasoned veteran of campaigns, I find most political speeches, whether standard stump speeches or scripted special events, turn me off. Even as someone who disagrees with him on many or most things, however, I find Trump's public events draw me in. I sit on the edge of my seat waiting to hear what he says next.

Trump understood that he could tap into growing popular rage at the political class. America faces fundamental challenges, if not an irreversible decline. And Americans are angry. Trump encapsulated better than anyone else the Republican rage that first became apparent in reaction to Obamacare with the birth of the Tea Party movement. He recognized he could build a campaign on anti-systemic politics and rhetoric.

Trump positioned himself, whether with immigration or Birtherism or traditional values or "America First," to be the person who was standing up for a displaced class in America. He is uniquely willing to say what he thinks, and damn the consequences. As is clear from the innumerable *Saturday Night Live* parodies of him, he really is the only person in American politics who speaks the way he speaks.

Conducting political surveys, I have spoken often and at length to the new Trump supporters. They are invariably older whites. What is most noticeable is that they feel a connection to him that goes beyond politics. It's not, "I support him." It's, "He's the last guy speaking for me. He says things that I think myself, and can't and haven't been able to articulate." It might seem a strange conclusion to those who like to tally up his lies, but to his followers he's "the last honest man."

NELSON MANDELA
President of South Africa 1994–1999;
President of the African National Congress 1991–1997,
and
THE DEMOCRATIC ALLIANCE

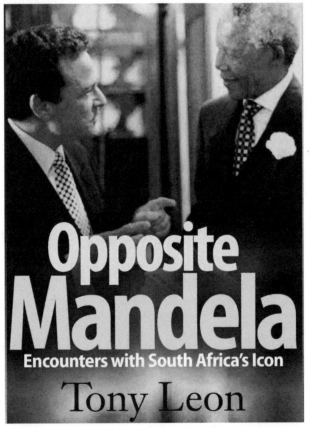

South African opposition leader Tony Leon had a friendly rivalry with anti-apartheid icon and former president Nelson Mandela, and wrote a book about it.

Truth 32

BUILD
YOUR BASE

You need to find a firm foothold before you climb a mountain. Make sure you identify the people you can rely upon from the start and keep them loyal to you.

I DON'T USUALLY talk much about how I once ran a campaign opposing Nelson Mandela.

The anti-apartheid hero, who spent twenty-seven years in prison for his cause, and became the first Black president of a free South Africa, is as close to a secular saint as it is possible to be. When people hear at dinner parties that I worked against Mandela's African National Congress and his chosen successor in the country's 1999 election, they immediately assume I am some kind of racist—which of course I am not. I was simply working for the new South Africa to become an open multi-party democracy, not a corrupt one-party state.

Mandela, who won the 1993 Nobel Peace Prize, never intended to serve more than one term as South Africa's president. In 1999, at the age of eighty, he announced he would not seek re-election and anointed his deputy, Thabo Mbeki, as the ANC candidate. Polling showed that while Mandela remained overwhelmingly popular, public support for the post-Mandela ANC was faltering.

I was introduced to South African politics by my old professor at Oxford University, R. W. "Bill" Johnson, a South African–born historian and journalist. After an academic career at Oxford, Johnson had gone back to South Africa to run the foundation set up by Helen Suzman, the Jewish activist who was for many years the only anti-apartheid campaigner in South Africa's whites-only Parliament (and for six years the only woman too).

When apartheid was overthrown, many white liberals were reluctant to level any criticism at the liberation movement for fear of being labeled reactionaries. This refusal to attack the ANC even for obvious corruption, for instance, became known as the "liberal slideaway." But the Democratic Party, of which Suzman had been a leading light, was determined to hold the ANC to account for its excesses.

After test polls and focus groups, we launched a campaign to challenge the ANC and its leader Mbeki under the slogan "Fight Back!" The idea was to encourage voters to "fight back" against corruption and malfeasance by the ANC government. But it also contained the idea that South Africa's whites and other ethnic minorities had to stand up for their rights under the new Black-majority rule.

The "Fight Back!" campaign, fronted by our presidential candidate, Tony Leon, sparked huge controversy. The ANC called it racist and responded with posters of their own declaring "Don't Fight Blacks."

"When apartheid was overthrown, many white liberals were reluctant to level any criticism at the liberation movement for fear of being labeled reactionaries."

In politics it was essential to build yourself a base. I argued that if the Democratic Party was to establish itself as an effective challenge to the ANC's corrosive monopoly on power, it needed a reliable coalition of supporters. Though Leon was Jewish and had roots in the same anti-apartheid Progessive Party that Suzman did, he needed to win over not just liberal English-speaking whites but also more conservative Afrikaners, as well as other minorities, while getting as many Black voters as possible.

The year 1999 was only the country's second democratic election—and Mbeki and the ANC won easily with 66 percent of the vote. But the Democratic Party multiplied its vote more than fivefold to almost 10 percent and increased its seats in the National Assembly from seven to thirty-eight. At the same time, the reincarnated New National Party, which had ruled during apartheid, saw its vote share fall by two-thirds and its seats cut from eighty-two to just twenty-eight. Its collapse meant the Democratic Party became the official opposition.

The successor Democratic Alliance is still the second-largest party in the National Assembly, now with 84 of the 400 seats to the ANC's 230. It also currently controls the country's second-largest city, Cape Town, and the surrounding Western Cape Province as well as Tshwane municipality, which includes the administrative capital, Pretoria. Mbeki's successor as ANC leader and president, Jacob Zuma, was forced from power by his own party amid corruption allegations and later went on trial for allowing the "state capture" of South Africa by a wealthy family of Indian origin. I am proud of my role. Now more than ever, the free South Africa needs a powerful and watchful opposition—so Mandela can rest in peace.

BILL CLINTON

President Clinton, on my advice, pivoted back to the center and signed welfare-reform into law, enabling him to win re-election in 1996.

Truth 33

TELL THEM WHAT THEY WANT TO HEAR

Friendship is founded on people agreeing with each other. It becomes hard to sustain if there is a fundamental disagreement between two people. So the easiest way to make and keep a friend is to tell them what they want to hear. They will love you for being just like them.

IT WAS THE FIRST TIME I had ever met a sitting US president. I was escorted into the White House for an audience with the most powerful man in the world. I had never met Bill Clinton in person, but I knew him to be a brilliant, charismatic, effervescent character. When I entered the room, I was shocked to find a man who was disconsolate, detached, and almost clinically depressed. Rather than being awed, I wanted to get up, grab him by the lapels, and physically shake him.

Clinton had won the presidency in 1992 as a "New Democrat" pledging to reform "welfare as we know it." But his administration quickly swung left to satisfy the new Democratic majority in Congress. Clinton ended the ban on gays in the military, replacing it with a policy of "Don't Ask, Don't Tell," and placed his wife, Hillary, in command of a radical reform of the US healthcare system. The Republicans responded with the "Contract with America," promising ten popular conservative policies that polled at over 60 percent approval, ranging from tax cuts to a Balanced Budget Amendment. (The contract cleverly omitted divisive issues like abortion and school prayer.)

In the 1994 midterms, the Republicans gained fifty-four House seats and nine Senate seats, winning control of both houses of Congress for the first time in forty years. The author of the Contract with America, Newt Gingrich, became Speaker of the House. At a press conference soon afterward, Clinton had to insist that, "The president is still relevant here." In his autobiography, *My Life*, he later confided: "I was profoundly distressed by the election, far more than I ever let on in public."

"Clinton clearly understood his problem. 'I'm way out of position,' he complained to me."

Diminished as he seemed when I met him, Clinton clearly understood his problem. "I'm way out of position," he complained to me. The centrist New Democrat who had won in 1992 with a slogan of, "It's the economy, stupid," had drifted out of touch with the American public who elected him. In telling the congressional Democrats what they wanted to hear, he had forgotten what American voters wanted to hear. If Clinton was to win re-election in 1996, it was the voters, not congresspeople, who were the crucial constituency. I was there to take remedial action.

Politicians are often criticized for pursuing policies based on polling and focus groups. It is seen as a sign of insincerity. But this is the way democracy is supposed to work. Democratically elected leaders are meant to respond to the wishes of the voters. Only when it veers into populism, when promises are made that cannot be kept, or favor the majority at the expense of the minority, does it become a problem.

I had started polling unofficially for Clinton after the electoral debacle. My first poll showed his approval rating well below 40 percent. It was clear to me he had to shed his image as a "tax-and-spend" liberal and card-carrying member of the "cultural elite" and reposition himself as a fiscal conservative who shared the values of American families.

My prescription at that first face-to-face meeting on February 6, 1995, was that he send a balanced budget to Congress. The idea met stiff resistance from liberals on the White House staff like Leon Panetta, Harold Ickes, and George Stephanopoulos. It garnered support, however, from powerful centrists such as Treasury Secretary Bob Rubin and Vice President Al Gore. Clinton finally announced it in a six-minute prime-time address to the nation on June 13, 1995 — pledging to balance the budget in ten years, three years sooner than the Republican plan. In fact, it was always pretty much inevitable Clinton would be presented with a balanced budget by the Republican Congress. This way, he got to define the terms. The Republicans twice shut down Congress to get their way. Clinton stood firm defending his choice to safeguard Medicare, Medicaid, education, and the environment — a quartet we dubbed "MMEE." For Clinton, the Republican shutdown of Congress proved a political bonanza.

Clinton also had to tell Americans what they wanted to hear on the cultural front. Our polling showed he suffered a "family gap," trailing the Republicans by up to 15 percent among married couples raising children. My brilliant partner Mark Penn told Clinton: "It's not about economics, it's about values." The Republicans' definition of "family values," focused on abortion, school prayer, and personal morality, was too restrictive for many voters. But the swing voters Clinton needed did want reassurance that their leader shared their broader values. Penn summarized them as the All-American values of "opportunity, responsibility, and community."

Clinton, a child of the South, made a speech defending school prayer within the bounds of the Constitution. He launched a spate of family-oriented policies such as keeping kids away from cigarettes, blocking violence on TV, instituting crime prevention programs, and improving America's schools. After rejecting the Republicans' original version, he signaled he would sign a revised welfare-reform bill. In his 1996 State of the Union address to Congress, Clinton boldly declared: "The era of big government is over."

His repositioning was complete. He was now telling an increasingly right-wing America what it wanted to hear. As history records, he was duly re-elected in November 1996.

FATHER LOU GIGANTE
Catholic Priest,
and
VINNIE "THE CHIN" GIGANTE
Mafia Boss

Father Louis Gigante, a Roman Catholic priest, right, walking in Greenwich village in New York City with his brother Vincente "The Chin" Gigante, the boss of the Genovese crime family, who feigned madness by going out in his pajamas. Lou made me a lucrative offer — but I refused.

Truth 34

REFUSE AN OFFER YOU CAN'T REFUSE

Not every opportunity is an opportunity, even if it promises to be very lucrative—indeed particularly if it promises to be very lucrative. Show discernment in assessing opportunities presented to you.

FATHER LOUIS GIGANTE was a popular "street priest" in the blighted South Bronx and my friend. His older brother Vincent was a Mafia don, the boss of one of New York's five crime families. Therein lay the problem.

Lou was the youngest of the five Gigante brothers, sons of a watchmaker and a seamstress who had emigrated from Naples to Greenwich Village. Like his big brothers, Lou was a tough, streetwise boy. An All-American athlete, he won a basketball scholarship to Georgetown University and captained the team to national success. As the Catholic priest at St. Athanasius Church in the South Bronx, he was renowned for walking his crime-ridden parish armed with a baseball bat.

Among his parishioners was a teenage Sonia Sotomayor, who would grow up to become the first Hispanic justice on the US Supreme Court. In her autobiography, *My Beloved World*, Sotomayor tells how her family was in awe of Lou's heroic struggle for the poor: "It wouldn't have occurred to me to call him a freedom fighter," she writes, "but why not?"

By the time I met him, Lou was already leading a tenants' rights movement. He had set up the South East Bronx Community Organization to build housing for the poor with federal money to replace the buildings being burned to the ground by arsonists. He has been credited by some with singlehandedly revitalizing the South Bronx. I was eighteen years old and a student at Harvard. I figured I could learn from him about a world I had never seen: poor people in the South Bronx. He was alleged to be part of organized crime. I had no idea then what that even was. I figured I'd get at least a window into a style of life, or, as his brother would put it, "The Life."

"Among his parishioners was a teenage Sonia Sotomayor, who would grow up to become the first Hispanic justice on the US Supreme Court."

Lou's big brother Vincent, or "Vinnie," had also started life as an athlete. In a short career as a light heavyweight boxer, he won sixteen of nineteen prizefights. Though known as "The Chin," the sobriquet came not from his fighting style but from his mother's affectionate Italian nickname for him, "Cinzino," pronounced "Chinzeeno." But Vinnie graduated to become a Mob enforcer for Lucky Luciano's crime family and a protegé of Vito Genovese, with whom he served five years in prison for heroin trafficking.

At age twenty-nine, Vinnie allegedly helped Genovese take over Luciano's criminal organization. Luciano's successor, Frank Costello, stepped down after a bullet grazed his head in the hallway of his building on Central Park West. Genovese assumed control. Vinnie was tried for attempted murder but acquitted when Costello testified he could not identify who shot him. On his way out of court, Vinnie was heard to say, "Thanks, Frank."

Vinnie would eventually take over himself as first the boss of what became known as the Genovese crime family. But he was, as a Mafia turncoat testified in court, "crazy as a fox." For decades, he pretended to be insane to keep law enforcement at bay. Every evening, he would emerge from his mother's home on Sullivan Street and walk around Greenwich Village in his bathrobe and pajamas. At night, FBI surveillance later revealed, he would be chauffeur-driven up to his mistress and his second family in a townhouse on the Upper East Side and dress up in much smarter togs. At breakfast, he would return home to Mom.

Despite his brother's notoriety, and the fact that at least two of his other brothers were involved with the Genovese crime family, Lou always denied any connection to organized crime. In fact, he even denied that the Mafia existed at all. The Mafia, he insisted to me, was a myth. His brothers simply had "friends" and he just wanted to do business with them. Although he kept me away from the details, it was clear to me that he wanted Vinnie's "friends" to do his construction work in the Bronx. He had, he explained, never taken a vow of poverty, and saw nothing incompatible in doing good work and at the same time making money. "Being a priest," he explained, "does not mean you cannot be a capitalist."

The first time I met Lou the brothers were, strangely, on opposite sides of a political race. It was the 1971 contest in which the "radical chic" Vanderbilt heir Carter Burden hoped to seize control of the New York Democratic Party, as we recounted in the earlier chapter "You Are Not Entitled." Vinnie and the Genovese crime family were backing the Tammany Hall incumbent for the key Democratic district leadership position in East Harlem, Frank Rossetti. I was working for the Reform challenger, Eugene Nardelli—and so, surprisingly, was Lou.

Lou explained the family split by saying he had "personal issues" with Rossetti, who had reneged on a promise to back him when he had run unsuccessfully for Congress in 1970. But it was very clear to me that the Genovese family was using its muscle on the street to back the incumbent against our challenger. It was only my second political campaign—and I discovered I was fighting not just Tammany Hall but also the Mob.

I was thrilled to get my candidate endorsed by Lou, who had won East Harlem overwhelmingly in his congressional race. Lou, however, was quite candid. "Those voters weren't for me," he explained. "They were for my friends in the neighborhood who were supporting me." That word "friends" again.

The Genovese gangster who ran East Harlem was a thug nicknamed "Buckaloo" who spent his days sitting in a beach chair chomping an unlit cigar outside a social club on 116th Street and Second Avenue. Buckaloo put out the word that he was supporting the incumbent, Rossetti. On election day, Rossetti's supporters were illegally campaigning inside polling stations. Despite my complaints, the police just shrugged.

The contest nevertheless forged an unlikely bond between me, the precocious prep school–educated Harvard freshman, and Lou Gigante, the baseball bat–wielding "street priest" and brother of a Mob boss. I never met Vinnie, who died in 2005, but I met two of the other brothers, Mario and Pasquale, known in English as "Pat," who had followed him into organized crime. I never had any doubt, however, that Lou was sincerely dedicated to his work for the downtrodden.

In 1973, I agreed to help Lou, the popular champion of the poor, run for New York City Council. While also incongruously working on the *Harvard Crimson* newspaper, I became his campaign manager. We won—Lou and I—by a slim 106 votes. Even with the help of the Genovese crime family, he wouldn't have won without me. I even arranged for him to come to Harvard to address the Kennedy School of Government.

Now Lou trusted me, which I learned was not necessarily a beneficial situation. When I was about to graduate from Harvard, he casually brought up my plans for the future. At the time, I was mulling whether to accept a fellowship to study politics at Oxford University. Lou suggested I just go straight to law school and, as soon as I was qualified, hang out a shingle and start my own firm. His family and "friends" could supply me with an inexhaustible flow of cases, he promised. "We know we can trust you," he confided.

It took me some years to fully understand the import of Lou's offer. He was effectively asking me to become a "House Counsel" for the Mob. It was the role played by Robert Duvall as Tom Hagen, consigliere to the fictional Corleone clan, in *The Godfather* movie, which had just come out. Having met some of these reputed Mob characters, I had come to learn that, quite apart from the casual attitude some had toward killing other people, these were just scary people. They may be efficacious, but they were certainly not people to casually mingle with. I'm sure Lou was sincere and that he meant well. He was trying to help me kickstart my career. Even at the age of twenty-one, though, I instinctively knew I was in deep enough. This was an offer I had to refuse. I chose Oxford over the Mob . . .

. . . but it did not end there. Some years later, Lou asked me for an introduction to my father, also a lawyer. I was proud to be able to bring business to my father, so I agreed. Lou went to dinner with my father and took along a "friend," Morris Levy. The sometime owner of the Birdland jazz club in Manhattan, Levy had once tried to trademark the term "Rock 'n' Roll." He became president of Roulette Records, responsible for such hits as "Peppermint Twist" and "Why Do Fools Fall in Love." Levy, who also opened a chain of Strawberries record stores, had been dogged by allegations of his Mob connections. The Sixties Rock 'n' Roller Tommy James, best known for his hit "Hanky Panky," later claimed Roulette Records was a front for the Genovese crime family and said Levy once threatened to throw him out the window. Levy was eventually sentenced to a ten-year term for extortion, but died before he was due to surrender to jail. I do not know what business Lou and Levy had with my father and my father volunteered nothing after their dinner. So I asked him. His only answer: "That was the scariest night of my life!"

SLOBODAN MILOŠEVIĆ
President of Yugoslavia 1997–2000, President of Serbia 1991–1997,
and
ME

The *"Bulldozer Revolution"* in Belgrade in 2000 ousted accused war criminal Slobodan Milošević.

Truth 35

THERE IS NO SUBSTITUTE FOR BOOTS ON THE GROUND

Power, in the end, boils down to people on the street. Whether it is the "ground game" and turnout in a democracy, or "people power" in a dictatorship, or military invasion and occupation in a war zone, you need to mobilize on-the-ground support.

WHEN I FIRST ARRIVED in the then-disintegrating Yugoslavia in 1992, I sought out the advice of a well-known intellectual about the political landscape. We arranged to meet at the historic Writer's Club in Belgrade, *Klub književnika*. As we sat down for dinner with his girlfriend, I remarked that I had been surprised by the number of people carrying guns on the streets and the "Check Your Guns at the Front Desk" sign at my hotel. He opened his jacket to reveal strap-on holsters holding two six-shooters that he could grab with either hand, like a *bandido* in the Wild West. As I said, this was an *intellectual*.

War had broken out in Yugoslavia as the ultra-nationalist leader of dominant Serbia battled to stop some of the smaller republics—Bosnia, Croatia, and Slovenia—from breaking away. My assignment was to rid the country and the world of the menace of Slobodan Milošević, the man who would come to be known as "The Butcher of the Balkans."

My first attempt failed. My second, eight years and an estimated 140,000 deaths later, succeeded.

As a political consultant, I specialize in "soft power." In Yugoslavia, I was to learn some hard lessons about "hard power."

We in America have a liberal assumption that everything can be negotiated, that if reasonable people can just sit down and talk they can be persuaded to reach a compromise. My experience in the wider world has taught me that is mostly BS. People are often unreasonable. They act in their own self-interest, and you should not trust what they say until you figure out what their self-interest is. People lie, cheat, and steal not because they are inherently dishonest, but because the rules of the game in many places are very different from the ones we Americans are brought up with. (Though perhaps not for much longer.)

My first bid to oust Milošević came in November 1992, just months after war erupted in Bosnia. I ran a highly unorthodox campaign for Milan Panić, the Serbian American founder of the successful American pharmaceutical company ICN. Panić was a former Yugoslav cycling champion who had defected from the Communist country on his way to a tournament in the Netherlands. He immigrated to California and became a US citizen, but remained committed to democracy and peaceful change in his homeland. Panić also remained committed, however, to the company he had built in America—and understandably did not want to lose his life.

"We in America have a liberal assumption that everything can be negotiated, that if reasonable people can just sit down and talk they can be persuaded to reach a compromise. My experience in the wider world has taught me that is mostly BS."

On election day, December 20, 1992, we conducted exit polls at sixty polling stations. They showed Panić ahead. The state media, all in Milošević's hands, reported a landslide for the dictator. Milošević simply stole the election.

I should have urged Panić to call his supporters onto the streets to protest, but I didn't have the experience to do so or, frankly, the nerve. And neither did he. Had we done so, we might have spared the Balkans years of genocidal warfare. We might, however, also have been killed.

Many years later, I saw Panić in New York and he apologized to me—not for failing to call his people onto the street, but for putting my life at risk. "Trust me," he said. "What I have subsequently learned is that our lives were always in danger."

By the time of my second campaign to dislodge Milošević in 2000, I had learned my lesson. By then, it was no longer safe for me to enter Serbia. I was *persona non grata*. So opposition leaders had to cross into neighboring Hungary to meet me secretly at the Marriott Hotel in Budapest.

Again, it was Panić who got me involved. "It's time to finish the job," he declared. I was working for an opposition coalition called the Alliance for Democratic Change put together with Panić's funding by a shrewd and eminently practical man named Zoran Djindjić, whose maverick personal journey had taken him from anarchism to liberalism to nationalism, and from academia to business to politics—and, some said, organized crime.

Once jailed as a student activist, Djindjić had moved to Germany to study with the leading neo-Marxist thinker Jurgen Habermas and became a ponytailed philosophy professor. He embraced Habermas's teaching that it was the duty of an intellectual not just to contemplate but also to act. While in Europe, Djindjić built a successful business importing machine tools from East Germany, leading to rumors of ties to the ubiquitous Balkan crime syndicates. He was a "can-do" guy.

The immediate problem was that our polling showed Djindjić was too unpopular to win an election. He didn't appreciate me telling him that, but his response was far-sighted. He proposed a much more popular minor-party leader and law professor, Vojislav Koštunica, as the candidate of a united opposition. "I can serve my purposes by making him the candidate," Djindjić candidly admitted. "And of course it will serve his purposes as well."

Stung by his near-death experience with Panić in 1992, Milošević had banned exit polling. So, instead, we dispatched observers to polling stations on election day—Sunday, September 24, 2000—to conduct what is called a "quick count," reporting real-time results. This time, we were able to announce victory before state TV, short-circuiting Milošević's effort to cheat again.

After several days of silence, the Milošević-controlled Federal Electoral Committee announced that neither candidate had won 50 percent of the vote and a runoff would be necessary. Unlike in 1992, we in the opposition were ready to take to the streets. Djindjić and others had been preparing for months.

On October 5, the growing student protest movement *Otpor!* ("Resistance") was joined by striking coal-miners and factory workers, as well as local mayors, including one with his own militia, in a mass demonstration in Belgrade. The crowds chanted our election slogan: *Gotov je! Gotov je!* ("He's finished! He's finished!). One protester drove a bulldozer up to the doors of the Milošević-controlled television station as the crowd seized control. Milošević conceded. "The Butcher of the Balkans" was finished—soon to face trial in the Hague for genocide. Dubbed "The Bulldozer Revolution," it was an awesome demonstration of that implacable force we now know as "people power."

Three years later, Djindjić was assassinated in broad daylight outside the main Serbian government building with a single shot from an assault rifle to the heart. The killing was ordered by a former special forces commander in Milošević's secret police who had joined organized crime. Panić was certainly correct when he told me that Balkan politics was dangerous and our lives were at risk—but we and the Serbian opposition had prevailed in the end.

PART FIVE

CONTROL YOUR ENEMIES

Enemies are only enemies as long as you do not control them. Once you do, they become useful tools.

DONALD TRUMP

Donald Trump launched his 2016 campaign by attacking Mexican immigrants as "rapists" and made his border wall, seen here in San Luis, Arizona, a symbol of his presidency.

Truth 36

PICK YOUR ENEMIES BEFORE THEY PICK YOU

Power is unfortunately often about the organization of hatred. It is easier to mobilize people against a common enemy than it is to rouse them in favor of a common cause. They say, you can't pick your enemies—but, oh yes, you can.

WHEN TRUMP DESCENDED his golden escalator at Trump Tower to launch his 2016 presidential bid, he delivered a now-famous tirade about Mexican immigrants. "When Mexico sends its people, they are not sending their best. . . . They are sending people who have lots of problems. They are bringing drugs. They are bringing crime. They are rapists. And some, I assume, are good people."

Later in the same speech, he announced his plan to build "a great Great Wall" along the United States' southern border and to make Mexico pay for it. By the end of his term, only forty miles of new primary wall and thirty-three miles of secondary wall had been built on the 1,954-mile frontier in locations where there had been no barrier before—and Mexico had not paid for any of it. But the policy had amply served its rallying purpose.

From the get-go, Trump had identified a common enemy—one of the best motivators known to mankind. Trump knows who the villains are—and they do not look like him or his predominantly white, male base. During his campaign and his presidency, he made enemies not just of commonplace targets like Mexican drug dealers, Islamic terrorists, or China. He also targeted NFL stars for "taking the knee" during the national anthem; women ranging from Cher ("Stop with the bad plastic surgery") to Rep. Maxine Waters ("An extraordinarily low-IQ person"); and even the disabled *New York Times* reporter Serge F. Kovaleski.

For Trump, and his backers, demonization represents empowerment. Trump has understood better than any other American politician today the deep-seated anger in the American electorate. Trolling is the spirit of the times. Rather than courting centrist voters, Trump has focused on turning out his base—an approach pioneered by Karl Rove for George W. Bush. By attacking establishment targets, Trump was able to bond with the alienated sections of the public even though he himself is part of that same rich and privileged white male elite.

Indeed, Trump has gone after pretty much anybody who has refused to pay homage to him. Even erstwhile Republican heroes Colin Powell ("a classic RINO, if even that") and John McCain ("He's not a war hero. He's a war hero because he was captured. I like people that weren't captured.") were not safe from his spite. At times, Trump acts like an aspiring rapper "dissing" rival stars to get attention.

His most reliable and rewarding target has been the media, aka the "Fake News Media" or the "LameStream Media" or simply "The Enemy of the People." In the crucial first Republican primary debate in 2015, Fox News moderator Megyn Kelly sought to land a knockout blow by challenging Trump: "You've called women you don't like 'fat pigs,' 'dogs,' 'slobs,' and 'disgusting animals.'" Trump somehow turned the question to his advantage with a joke at the expense of an old talk-show nemesis. "Only Rosie O'Donnell," he quipped. Game, set, and match, Trump. In the days that followed, Trump mounted a retaliatory offensive against Kelly. "There was blood coming out of her eyes, blood coming out of her wherever," he claimed.

> **"By the end of his term, only forty miles of new primary wall and thirty-three miles of secondary wall had been built on the 1,954-mile frontier in locations where there had been no barrier before—and Mexico had not paid for any of it."**

As president, Trump routinely attacked high-profile journalists such as MSNBC's Rachel Maddow and Joe Scarborough, NBC's Chuck Todd, CNN's Chris Cuomo, and Maggie Haberman of the *New York Times*. The US Press Freedom Tracker, which maintains a database of Trump's insults to journalists, says he has denounced the media more than 2,000 times—an average of at least once a day throughout his presidency. But what the public too often fails to appreciate is that once he is done bashing the "Fake News Media" publicly, Trump is often schmoozing with those very same journalists.

From Trump's first gambit in politics—placing national newspaper ads in 1987 demanding America's allies contribute to the defense of the Persian Gulf shipping lanes—he had already settled on his nativist "America First" theme.

That xenophobia has often shaded into racism. From my contact with Trump, I do not believe he is an outright racist. He does not believe in the innate inferiority of non-white people. Nor is he uncomfortable having them around him. He is someone from the New York suburbs of the 1950s when people spoke about "Jewish guys" and "Italian guys" with occasional ethnic slurs, the way comedians of that era would tell jokes. That said, Trump is definitely someone who will manipulate race to his personal benefit with no qualms or hesitation. He is, in a dastardly way, brilliant at it. Already back in 1989, he took out full-page ad in four New York newspapers to raise his profile by calling for the reintroduction of the death penalty after five Black and Hispanic youths were convicted—wrongly, it turned out—of the infamous "wilding" Central Park rape. Deal Trump a Race Card and he will happily play it to win.

Trump figured out that the explicit use of racial symbolism, short of outright racist denigration, was a very effective political tool. Nowhere is this clearer than in his boosting of so-called "Birtherism," the frankly preposterous theory that Hawaii-born president Obama was not born in the United States and was therefore prohibited by the Constitution from holding the highest office. This spurious fringe idea was first promoted by Trump and his backers at the *National Enquirer* supermarket tabloid when he flirted with running against Obama in the 2012 election—a clear prelude to a campaign that never took place. In the 2020 campaign, Trump sought to transfer that "Birtherism" onto Kamala Harris, suggesting she might not qualify to become vice president because of the immigration status of her Jamaican father and Indian mother at the time of her birth. The *Newsweek* article that floated the bogus theory was written by John Eastman, the same conservative law professor who later penned a memo proposing Trump had the power to overturn the 2020 election result.

Does Trump believe in "Birtherism" or "Stop the Steal"? In person, he is an astute man. He knows perfectly well what he is doing. He just doesn't care. When a Big Lie is convenient for him, he will convince himself there is something to it. He is unscrupulous in the mobilization of hate—and in this world there is always more than enough hatred to go around.

KIM DAE-JUNG

Kim Dae-jung, President of South Korea 1998–2003

NEWSMAKERS / GETTY IMAGES

South Korean president Kim Dae-jung, right, cozied up to North Korean leader Kim Jong-il at a historic three-day summit in Pyongyang in June 2000 even though their countries were still in a state of war.

Truth 37

MANAGE THE COMPETITION

See your enemy as a resource, who can be turned against other enemies. Because you rarely have only one enemy at a time. The "enemy of my enemy" does not have to be a "friend." They just need to be useful.

KIM DAE-JUNG was once hailed as the "Mandela of Asia." Like South Africa's anti-apartheid hero Nelson Mandela, he also won a Nobel Peace Prize. But having lost to him in South Korea's 1997 election, I can tell you that he was a formidable political operator with an uncanny ability to manipulate friends and foes alike.

Kim, known in the country of relatively few surnames simply by the initials of his given name, "DJ," was South Korea's leading pro-democracy dissident in the decades of dictatorship that followed the Korean War. He was elected to the National Legislature for the first time just a week before the 1961 coup that propelled Major General Park Chung-hee to power, and for the duration of Park's rule DJ became the greatest thorn in his side.

In 1973, as DJ assembled a pro-democracy coalition in exile, Korean Central Intelligence Agency (KCIA) spies kidnapped him from his hotel room in Tokyo, Japan, and spirited him out of the country on a fishing boat. They had already chained concrete blocks to him and were about to dump him into the sea when the United States intervened to save his life. In 1980, he was sentenced to death for treason—only to be saved again by the United States, where he took refuge for three years.

Undeterred, DJ ran repeatedly for president. The 1997 election was his fourth attempt to enter the presidential Blue House. A farmer's son from poor Cholla province in the southwest, he remained an outsider in South Korean politics. But he proved masterful at managing his rivals in the country's faction-ridden political scene.

My candidate in the 1997 poll was Lee Hoi-chang, the scion of an elite family who had become the youngest-ever chief justice of the country's Supreme Court. Lee's reputation for honesty in South Korea's notoriously corrupt politics was such that he was nicknamed the "Bamboo," a man of upright moral principle. As a judge, he had taken a stand against the armed forces trying civilians before military courts. Later, as chairman of the National Election Commission, he launched investigations into corruption by the ruling party.

I thought Chairman Lee, as everyone called him, was an excellent candidate: impeccably qualified, extremely popular, and unquestionably honest. A pro-business conservative, he took a tough stance on the threat from the

Communist menace from North Korea, which had remained in a state of war with the South since the Armistice of 1953.

We were, however, outmaneuvered. For all his virtues, Chairman Lee had not just the moral fiber but also unfortunately the public demeanor of a bamboo. His delivery was so stiff that I considered him a South Korean Al Gore. As a political operator, the veteran activist Kim Dae-jung was just light years shrewder.

Chairman Lee was the candidate of the ruling New Korea Party. But the incumbent president, Kim Young-sam—known as "YS"—was dogged by a reputation for corruption. We made a bold power play to merge with a smaller party headed by a former mayor of Seoul—despite a strong personal rivalry—to distance ourselves from YS and create a new grouping with a new name: The Grand National Party.

South Korean politics is a kaleidoscope of factions dominated by individual politicians. Before I arrived, Chairman Lee had taken a big hit in the polls when it emerged that his two sons had avoided the military draft by apparently starving themselves so they turned up emaciated at their Army physicals. Our new political alliance propelled him back into contention.

However, Kim Dae-jung had tricks of his own up his sleeve. They were totally brilliant—and totally nefarious.

Kim Dae-jung, or "DJ," and Kim Young-sam, or "YS," were two of the so-called "Three Kims" in South Korean politics. The third was Kim Jong-pil, or "JP." As a young intelligence officer, JP had helped to plot the coup that brought his friend Park Chung-hee to power in 1961. He also founded the Korean Central Intelligence Agency, which had kidnapped Kim Dae-jung in Tokyo on Park's orders in 1973.

Their unhappy history—which almost saw DJ tossed into the Sea of Japan—mattered little in the contest for power. Nor did their current policies. JP was a Cold Warrior on North Korea; DJ sought friendly relations with the Communist hardliners north of the border. All that mattered was that JP, a ruthless political kingmaker who had previously served as the dictator Park's prime minister, controlled a sizable bloc of conservative voters. It takes some nerve to recruit as an ally a man whose intelligence services once tried to kill you. Yet DJ was happy to welcome his old enemy JP to his side.

It takes even more nerve to recruit someone whose stated aim is the obliteration of your entire country. Yet DJ also cozied up to the tyrant in North Korea, Kim Jong-il (the father of the current North Korean leader). Despite the continued state of war, DJ proclaimed a "Sunshine Policy" aimed at reconciliation with North Korea. The North had been raising tension for months, sending soldiers into the Demilitarized Zone and ships into South Korean waters, assassinating a prominent defector and a South Korean diplomat in Vladivostok, and even threatening a critical South Korean newspaper with "extermination." By intimidating South Koreans, North Korea's threats served DJ's interests.

"It takes even more nerve to recruit someone whose stated aim is the obliteration of your entire country."

DJ, with the help of two apparent enemies, pipped Chairman Lee to a narrow victory amid the turmoil of the Asian economic crisis. JP, the wily old intelligence agent, became prime minister. In 2000, DJ held the first-ever North–South summit with North Korean leader Kim Jong-il in Pyongyang. The summit and DJ's "Sunshine Policy" won him the 2000 Nobel Peace Prize.

Only later did it emerge that North Korea had received at least $100 million from Kim Dae-jung's government through the South Korean conglomerate Hyundai as an apparent bribe to hold the summit. The Hyundai heir Chung Mong-hun, whose father founded the group, was charged with altering the company accounts to disguise the payments. Before he could stand trial he jumped to his death from his twelfth-floor office. By then, the "Sunshine Policy" and the North–South summit had already served Kim Dae-jung's purposes.

OPPOSITION RESEARCH AND THE "PEE TAPE"

Real-life James Bond Christopher Steele, a former MI6 agent, compiled the dubious dossier on Donald Trump in the 2016 campaign that included salacious allegations of a "pee tape."

Truth 38

PLAY OFFENSE

It is an immutable feature of power that if you are on the attack, you are not being attacked; and if you are not on the attack, you are susceptible to being attacked yourself. Protect yourself by attacking first.

THE SEXUAL PROCLIVITIES of presidents have always been a staple of US politics. Thomas Jefferson was accused of having sex with the enslaved Sally Hemings and fathering at least one of her children; Grover Cleveland was alleged to have fathered a child by rape; Warren Harding was said to have sired a child with a mistress with whom he had sex in a closet off the Oval Office; and then there was the failed impeachment of Bill Clinton.

No previous allegations, however, had ever been quite so lurid as those against Donald Trump in a dossier published online by *Buzzfeed News* on January 10, 2017, just weeks after he won the election.

"TRUMP'S (perverted) conduct in Moscow included hiring the presidential suite of the Ritz Carlton Hotel, where he knew President and Mrs. OBAMA (whom he hated) had stayed on one of their official trips to Moscow, and defiling the bed where they had slept by employing a number of prostitutes to perform a 'Golden Showers' (urination) show in front of him. The hotel was known to be under FSB control with microphones and concealed cameras in all the main rooms to record anything they wanted to."

This breathtaking claim formed part of a dossier prepared by a former British spy named Christopher Steele, which had been circulating in Washington for weeks. The suggestion that Russia's FSB intelligence service had videotaped this *kompromat* (comprising material) played into a wider narrative that Trump was colluding with Moscow. Trump immediately denounced the dossier on Twitter as "FAKE NEWS—A TOTAL POLITICAL WITCH HUNT!" At first I, like many, dismissed his claim that he had been set up. In light of what has come out since, I tend now to agree with him.

"In my experience, it is unprecedented for opposition research to commission work by former foreign intelligence agents."

Opposition research, colloquially known as "oppo research," has become an essential ingredient of the democratic struggle for power. It is one of the first things candidates do in their campaign. As a first priority, you have to identify your own vulnerabilities and your opponents' Achilles' heel. To deflect attacks against yourself, you must relentlessly attack your opponents' weaknesses.

It used to be a simple matter of making a background check in public records to see if your rival had committed any crimes or gone bankrupt or owed any child support. If the opponent was involved in any business deals gone bad or had any unsavory friends or associates, they might be tarred with "guilt by association." Their previous votes and public statements would be scoured, back to their student days, for any embarrassing remarks or inconsistent positions. These days, candidates are constantly pursued by camera-toting "trackers" who videotape anything they say in the hope of catching a gaffe.

The Steele Dossier prepared for the 2016 campaign, and its sensational claim that Russia had a compromising "pee tape" of the new president, proved, however, to be opposition research run amok.

The dossier was in fact the work product of Hillary Clinton's campaign, which hired the Perkins Coie law firm, which in turn commissioned "opposition research" on Trump by the commercial research firm Fusion GPS, set up by former *Wall Street Journal* reporters Glenn Simpson and Peter Fritsch. Fusion GPS turned to Steele, a former longtime Russia specialist in Britain's MI6 intelligence agency who had established his own private research firm called Orbis Business Intelligence.

In my experience, it is unprecedented for opposition research to commission work by former foreign intelligence agents. It is also unprecedented that a campaign would leverage "oppo research" to try to provoke an FBI investigation.

The Steele Dossier was shown to journalists in Washington and presented to the FBI ahead of the 2016 election to try to get them to probe Trump's alleged "collusion" with Russia. It was actually used by the FBI to get intelligence wiretaps on Trump's former campaign adviser Carter Page.

The subsequent investigation of Trump's Russia links by Special Counsel Robert Mueller reported numerous connections but stopped short of finding any actual conspiracy between the Trump campaign and Russia. Mueller ignored the mind-boggling charges in the Steele Dossier as unsubstantiated. However, a further inquiry, set up by Trump, by Special Counsel John Durham found serious flaws in Steele's methodology.

Steele had obtained much of his information through a US-resident Russian analyst, Igor Danchenko, who had once worked for the Brookings Institution in Washington. Danchenko served as a "collector" of information, including the tip about the supposed "pee tape," from other sources to which he had access. But Danchenko has now been charged with lying to the FBI about his contacts with those alleged sources.

Of particular note was Danchenko's relationship with Charles Dolan Jr., a PR man whose firm had represented the Russian government and the state-owned Gazprom oil company. Despite his extensive Russian connections, Dolan also had deep roots in Hillaryland, having served as a state chairman for Bill Clinton's 1992 and 1996 campaigns and acted as an adviser to Hillary in her 2008 race and a volunteer in her 2016 campaign.

Danchenko was charged with lying to the FBI when he denied receiving information for the Steele Dossier from Dolan. The indictment notes that Dolan had toured the presidential suite at the Ritz-Carlton Moscow in June 2016 and met the hotel's general manager, a female staff member, and other hotel staff—all of whom were cited in the dossier. Danchenko met Dolan in Moscow on June 14, 2016; he flew to London three days later on June 17, 2016; and the section of the dossier on the "pee tape" was written three days after that on June 20, 2016.

It was not clear from the indictment whether Dolan ever told Danchenko anything about the alleged "Golden Showers," or whether Danchenko just made it up, or whether it was simply Russian disinformation fed into the system. Danchenko says he told Steele it was just unconfirmed "rumor and speculation."

What is clear is that Dolan insisted to the FBI that individuals affiliated with the Hillary Clinton campaign "did not direct, and were not aware of" his dealings with Danchenko. Any knowledge by any Hillary Clinton aides would indeed be explosive—and to date there has been absolutely no showing of any contacts with the Hillary Clinton camp.

DONALD TRUMP

Donald J. Trump ✔
@realDonaldTrump

People are disgusted and embarrassed by the Fake News Media, as headed by the @nytimes, @washingtonpost, @comcast & MSDNC, @ABC, @CBSNews and more. They no longer believe what they see and read, and for good reason. Fake News is, indeed, THE ENEMY OF THE PEOPLE!

4:13 PM · Mar 1, 2020 · Twitter for iPhone

Donald Trump attacks the "Fake News Media" in one of the more than 25,000 tweets he posted during his presidency.

Truth 39

COMMUNICATE TO DOMINATE

The goal of power is always to control the narrative. In our always-on social media culture, that means defining your enemies and constantly driving the conversation.

"DRAIN THE SWAMP," "Lock Her Up," "Stop the Steal." Three words for a slogan. "Crooked Hillary," "Sleepy Joe." Just two words for a strategic insult.

Donald Trump has pioneered a new mode of communication in American politics for our new "attention economy," where the competition for the consumer's interest is paramount. Just as John F. Kennedy became the first American president of the television era, so Trump was the first president of the "social media" age.

President Kennedy broke through in the first-ever televised presidential debates in 1960, watched by almost 70 million Americans. One poll, conducted by Sindlinger & Co, found that Kennedy "won" the debate 43 to 20 percent among television viewers while Nixon "won" 28 to 19 percent among radio listeners. Though probably too limited itself to justify the sweeping conclusion, the poll spawned the idea that "Kennedy won on image." This triggered the popular but flippant "hair theory" of presidential elections that the candidate with the best hair always wins.

Trump has created his own political vocabulary and way of communicating. What Trump understood, and what got him elected, is the key concept of tweeting and control. In the attention economy, it is vital to dominate the public conversation.

When I was in the White House as a political adviser in the Clinton years, we spent the bulk of our time trying to "control the narrative." The problem every day was: How do we "win" the day? Frequently, Bill Clinton lost the day. Donald Trump, by dint of tweeting, good, bad, or indifferent, won virtually every day. He controlled the narrative in the social media dialogue every day. And since it was not encumbered by a commitment to veracity or integrity, it didn't matter if what he said was strictly speaking the truth. Indeed, he also learned that hyperbole, even if—indeed especially if—it involved vicious ad hominem attacks, almost certainly guaranteed him control. His view was that dominance of the channels of communication was more important than what you communicated. It was a new theory of presidential communications that virtually no one else understood.

Trump is a tabloid headline-writer manqué. When I worked with him in the 1980s, other politicians were scrutinizing the *New York Times*. His principal daily read was the brassy *New York Post*. He relished the fact he was dubbed "The Donald" in tabloid-speak, with its echoes of being a Mafia don. At the time, the *Post* called real-life Mafia Godfather John Gotti "The Dapper Don." He was trying to create an image of himself as a man who was the Boss—an image he later had even more success projecting on *The Apprentice*. He understood before anyone else in New York that branding was more important than anything else.

> ## "Trump is a tabloid headline-writer manqué. When I worked with him in the 1980s, other politicians were scrutinizing the *New York Times*. His principal daily read was the brassy *New York Post*."

The New York tabloids were his world. His divorce from Ivana made the front page of the tabloids eleven days in a row. They both had their own gossip columnist: Ivana trusted Liz Smith of the *New York Daily News*; Trump relied on Cindy Adams of the *Post*. That is how they communicated with each other. Even back then it was obvious that Trump had realized that hyperbole and bombast was an efficacious way to proceed. When the *Daily News* ran a front-page story sympathetic to Ivana one day, he called up Jerry Nachman, the editor of the *Post*, to demand a retaliatory banner headline. The worldly Nachman explained that he could not just demand a front-page story; there actually had to be a good story. According to *Post* TV columnist Jill Brooke, who was listening on speakerphone in the editor's office, Trump asked what gets a front-page story. "It's usually murder, money, or sex," Nachman informed him. Not losing a beat, Trump responded: "Marla says with me it's the best sex she's ever had!" Nachman, delighted, said he would of course need corroboration. "Marla, didn't you say it's the best sex you ever had with me?" Trump yelled to someone else in the room. Over the speakerphone came a faint voice agreeing: "Yes, Donald." The next morning the *Post*'s front page screamed in bold type: "Best Sex I've Ever Had."

It was a classic tabloid headline and remains one of Trump's greatest PR feats. And it must have been particularly hurtful to Ivana. He never had any compunction about exaggeration, cruelty, or lying. He was willing to say whatever it took to make the sale.

Trump found his tabloid communication skills particularly well adapted to Twitter. His Twitter following had ballooned to 88.7 million by the time he was thrown off the platform for inciting violence after the 2020 election. He tweeted more than 25,000 times during his presidency—an average of eighteen times a day. His longest break: just 1.9 days in June 2017 during former FBI Director James Comey's testimony to Congress.

Trump's hallmark has been the pithy two-word epithet for his opponents: "Crooked Hillary," "Sleepy Joe." The *New York Times* traced the rhetorical technique back to Homer, where every major character in the *Iliad* and the *Odyssey* is identified by a distinctive adjective. It rather grandly called Trump's Twitter technique the "Homeric adjective"—and that's Homer as in Ancient Greece, not *The Simpsons*.

The first American politician to receive such a "Homeric" moniker was "Tricky Dicky" Nixon. Intriguingly, it was Nixon, and more particularly his wife, Pat, who first spotted Trump's presidential potential after watching him in a "tabloid TV" format. In a two-sentence note in December 1987, Nixon told Trump his wife, Pat, had seen him on the Phil Donahue TV talk show and thought he did "great," with the word "great" underlined by hand, just as Trump himself might have done. "As you can imagine, she is an expert on politics and she predicts that whenever you decide to run for office you will be a winner!" Nixon declared. Trump framed the letter and put it on display in his office in Trump Tower.

Trump, of course, flourished as the Reality TV star of *The Apprentice*, an unlikely hit in which an oft-bankrupted businessman presumed to give business advice to others. His catchphrase was: "You're fired!" The command positioned him perfectly in the popular imagination to deliver the same message to the political establishment when he ran for president in 2016—and most particularly to the former First Lady who many saw as exploiting her insider status to try to become president herself. Trump served as a proxy for the many Americans who simply wanted to scream at Hillary: "You're fired!"

By the time he hit on "Crooked Hillary," Trump had already deployed his two-word put-downs to demolish a field of Republican primary challengers, including "Lyin' Ted" Cruz, "Little Marco" Rubio, and "Low Energy" Jeb

Bush. "Crooked Hillary" played on her reputation as untrustworthy and manipulative. "It works," he told the *New York Times*. "It flows." Again, there was a Nixonian echo. Nixon effectively committed public suicide when he volunteered to the press at Disney World on November 17, 1973, the fatal words: "I am not a crook." The "Crooked Hillary" moniker seemed designed to lure Hillary into a similar "I am not crooked" reply. Soon crowds were chanting "Lock Her Up."

Trump boasts a preternatural ability to identify an opponent's weakness. These snappy monikers — "Crooked Hillary," "Sleepy Joe" — define his rivals solely by that weakness. He has mobilized this attack against everyone from "Crazy" Bernie Sanders and "Pocahontas" Elizabeth Warren to "Leakin'" James Comey and "Little Rocket Man" Kim Jong-un. Few people have stumped him, except perhaps former longtime Trump loyalist and Senate Majority Leader Mitch McConnell. Trump's sobriquet for McConnell has been sliding around between "Old Crow," "Broken Old Crow," and "Old Broken Crow."

The truly remarkable aspect of Trump's bullet-like communication is the fact that no one has yet come up with a two-word epithet for him that has stuck, apart from the laudatory "The Donald." He is virtually bulletproof. This lack of a single pejorative moniker shows how totally Trump dominates the field. No one can name him because he owns the naming game.

ALEXANDRIA OCASIO-CORTEZ

Alexandria Ocasio-Cortez, who would become America's youngest-ever congresswoman, dancing for a student video while at Boston University. She later blamed the Republicans' fixation on her on "deranged sexual frustrations."

Truth 40

LET NO ATTACK GO UNANSWERED

An attack that goes unanswered is a successful attack. While you might wish to turn the other cheek, you must engage. Do not give space to your enemies, and act promptly so that calumnies do not take hold.

THE DAY BEFORE Alexandria Ocasio-Cortez was sworn in as the youngest-ever congresswoman, a right-wing Twitter account posted an old video of her dancing. The clip showed her strutting her stuff with other Boston University students on a rooftop eight years earlier as a tongue-in-cheek tribute to the mass dancing scene in the film *The Breakfast Club*. "Here is America's favorite commie know-it-all acting like the clueless nit-wit she is," the now-deleted Twitter account proclaimed. The clip quickly went viral, garnering more than 5 million views.

Far from being intimidated, the freshman congresswoman quickly hit back with a new Twitter clip of herself—dancing at the door of her office at the House of Representatives. "I hear the GOP thinks women dancing are scandalous," she tweeted. "Wait till they find out Congresswomen dance too!"

"Ocasio-Cortez, whose red-bearded boyfriend, Riley Roberts, is a web developer, comes from a social media generation and has the web savvy and the following to out-meme any of her trolls."

Political campaigns have long set up rapid-reaction teams to respond quickly to negative stories, lest they take hold in the public's mind. Giant corporations have increasingly followed this model to keep themselves on offense in the twenty-four-hour news cycle. But social media has multiplied the threat a thousandfold—and made it simultaneously easier for politicians to respond. AOC, as she is now commonly known, is a fish in water.

Social media has enabled users to wage asymmetrical warfare against politicians. One troll can quickly reach an audience of millions. But Ocasio-Cortez, whose red-bearded boyfriend, Riley Roberts, is a web developer, comes from a social media generation and has the web savvy and the following to out-meme any of her trolls.

From the moment she was elected in 2018, Ocasio-Cortez has faced relentless online criticism not just for her Leftist politics but also for clothes and behavior—and even her boyfriend's shaggy look.

When she suggested that she would struggle to pay the rent on new lodgings in Washington until she got her first paycheck as a congresswomen, Twitter critics circulated a photo shot from behind of her wearing seemingly expensive clothes. (They were apparently unaware a friend had bought her a subscription to Rent-the-Runway clothes-rental service.) Ocasio-Cortez mocked the *Washington Examiner* reporter who first posted the image. "If I walked into Congress wearing a sack, they would laugh and take a picture of my backside," she tweeted. "If I walk in with my best sale-rack clothes, they laugh and take a picture of my backside."

After he made a brief appearance in the documentary *Knock Down the House*, a political journalist criticized Ocasio-Cortez's boyfriend for looking like a "bin raccoon." Ocasio-Cortez good-humoredly posted a fresh photo showing him with a new haircut. "The internet roasted Riley into getting a haircut/glow-up," she laughed.

AOC seems to be getting even bolder in her counterattacks. When she was photographed eating lunch maskless outside in Miami with her boyfriend in sandals during the pandemic, former Trump adviser Steve Cortes tweeted the image. "1. If Leftists like AOC actually thought mandates and masking worked, they wouldn't be frolicking in free FL," Cortes complained. "2. Her guy is showing his gross pale male feet in public (not at a pool/beach) with hideous sandals."

Ocasio-Cortez's response in a quick-fire series of tweets was a classic put-down: "If Republicans are mad they can't date me they can just say that instead of projecting their sexual frustrations onto my boyfriend's feet. Ya creepy weirdos . . . It's starting to get old ignoring the very obvious, strange, and deranged sexual frustrations that underpin the Republican fixation on me, women, & LGBT+ people in general . . . These people clearly need therapy, won't do it, and use politics as their outlet instead. It's really weird."

Weirdly, indeed, Ocasio-Cortez is like Trump in her mastery of social media. Although political opposites, both are "movement politicians" who speak unfiltered to their supporters. Ocasio-Cortez has 12.8 million followers on Twitter—more than any other member of Congress, with Nancy Pelosi a distant second at 7.3 million. If he were still on Twitter, even Trump—who once tweeted "AOC is a Wack Job!"—would struggle to find an answer to her audacious riposte that the Republicans who criticize her really just want to have sex with her.

RECEP TAYYIP ERDOĞAN

President of Turkey 2014–, Prime Minister of Turkey 2003–2014

Turkish president Recep Tayyip Erdoğan built a mosque in Istanbul's main Taksim Square and inaugurated it at Friday Prayers on May 28, 2021.

Truth 41

KNOW WHERE THE OTHER GUY IS HEADED

If you are going to counter your opponent's next move, you must know what it is—just like chess. Study your enemy's game so that you understand his strategy.

IN 1994, I FOUGHT a municipal election for mayor in Istanbul, Turkey. If you think that sounds inconsequential, you would be tragically wrong. The result determined the fate of a major regional power and NATO ally—and continues to affect conflicts from Azerbaijan to Libya, from Syria to Ukraine to this day.

And I knew even then that it would.

My client was an ethnically Kurdish engineer named Bedrettin Dalan who was famous in Turkey for his azure blue eyes. Dalan had served as Istanbul mayor once before, when he became known for his pledge to clean up the city's stinking waterways so that "the waters of the Golden Horn will be the same color as my eyes." He had embarked on far-reaching urban renewal projects, including building a highway up the shore of the Bosporos that opened up new stretches of forest to development. But he earned a fearsome reputation for corruption, becoming so rich that he later endowed a foundation and a new university. At his second attempt, he was defeated by a Leftist. In 1994, Dalan was attempting a comeback for the governing center-right True Path Party of Tansu Çiller, Turkey's first-ever female prime minister.

The rival candidate who scared us was not a Leftist but another outsider, a forty-year-old working-class Islamist renowned for his public speaking named Recep Tayyip Erdoğan. To those who follow world politics, the name might be familiar. He has been the undisputed leader of Turkey now for twenty years.

"He built himself a 1,000-room presidential palace—and appears to have no plans to move out."

Erdoğan came from a poor neighborhood on the banks of the foul-smelling Golden Horn that Dalan promised to clean up. As a boy, he was a street hawker who sold *simit*, a kind of sesame-covered Turkish bagel. Educated at an Islamic school, where he was recognized for his ability to recite poetry, he had become a protégé of Turkey's preeminent Islamist leader, Necmettin Erbakan.

Turkey is the successor to the 600-year Ottoman Empire whose emperor claimed to be the Caliph of the Islamic world. The country had been re-founded as a secular republic by Mustafa Kemal Atatürk in 1923. The Turkish military and ruling establishment had long battled to keep Islam out of politics. Erbakan, the leading Islamist, was periodically banned from politics before renaming his party and starting again.

It was immediately clear to me that Erdoğan, the Islamist candidate for mayor, represented a real threat not just to Istanbul but to the whole future of Turkey. We focused our mayoral campaign on that threat. One TV ad we aired showed a secular elementary school fading from the screen and being replaced by a religious *madrassa*. I thought it was a powerful ad, but it had zero impact. Turks were demonstrating in the street to save their fellow Bosnian Muslims from genocide. The economy was in bad shape and Çiller's True Path party was in power, and so attracted the blame. More importantly, the electorate was so infuriated by corruption of Çiller's party that no other issue could cut through. Even though we could see clearly where Erdoğan was heading, we totally failed to convince the Turkish public, much less Turkey's Western allies, of the danger an Islamist victory posed.

Erdoğan, the outsider Islamist candidate, won the Istanbul mayoralty with just 25 percent of the vote. The center-right vote was split with one candidate coming in second with 22 percent and our guy, Dalan, in fourth with 15 percent. It was Erdoğan's first elected office.

Within three years, both Erdoğan and his mentor Erbakan were forced out of politics in one of Turkey's periodic crackdowns on Islamists. Erdoğan spent four months in jail for incitement for reciting an Islamic poem hinting at *jihad*: "The mosques are our barracks, the domes our helmets, the minarets our bayonets, and the faithful our soldiers." But he renamed the Islamist party once again and bounced back to win election as prime minister in 2002.

He has been in power ever since, eventually rewriting the constitution to become an all-powerful president. Giant mosques worthy of the Ottoman sultans have been built on a hill above the Bosphorus and in Istanbul's main Taksim Square. Thousands of his political opponents have been jailed. Though once promising that religion would play the same role in Turkish politics that it does in Germany—home to many Turkish guest-workers— with the Christian Democrats, he has turned his back on what was once called the "Turkish model" of moderate Islam. Instead, he has governed with a brand of kleptocratic Islamism and harbors pretensions to reconstruct the

Ottoman Empire. He built himself a 1,000-room presidential palace—and appears to have no plans to move out.

Erdoğan is known in Turkey for his quote as mayor: "Democracy is like a tram. You ride it until you arrive at your destination, then you step off." In 1994, we were riding the same democracy tram and we saw where our fellow passenger planned to disembark. But the other passengers did not. I now realize that you can know where your enemy is going—but you cannot necessarily stop him from getting there.

"DEFUND THE POLICE"

After days of protests over the killing of George Floyd, a section of 16th Street near the White House was renamed "Black Lives Matter Plaza."

Truth 42

PEOPLE ONLY DO BAD WHEN THEY THINK THEY ARE DOING GOOD

You will never understand your enemy if you just assume they are a bad person. Almost no one sets out to be evil. Instead, they have a rationale for why what they are doing is good. You have to understand their logic before you can defeat it.

THE EXCRUCIATING cell phone video of George Floyd being asphyxiated for nine minutes and twenty-nine seconds by a police officer kneeling on his neck in 2020 triggered a cathartic moment of collective outrage in America. It provoked violent riots and the largest ever wave of peaceful demonstrations in our nation's history. The clear-cut police brutality—which led to the murder conviction of Officer Derek Chauvin—spurred a chorus of emotional calls to "defund the police."

The campaign had already been percolating with Black activists in Minneapolis after a string of police shootings of young Black men. When Floyd was also killed in the city, these activists made "defunding the police" their central demand. A crowd staged a sit-in in the street outside the home of Mayor Jacob Frey to demand the abolition of the Minneapolis Police Department. When he refused, he was jeered back inside—and the video clip went viral.

The "defund the police" protesters undoubtedly had good intentions. They thought they were going to move money from the police force into community services that would magically lift people up and make crime disappear. As if it were that easy . . . The notion was at best utopian; more likely, it was simply foolish.

"Victims of crime do not want to 'defund the police.'"

"Defund the police" might be dear to the heart of Progressives who represent poor, diverse districts. But it is not dear to the hearts of their voters. Victims of crime do not want to "defund the police." Polling shows that minority voters might believe police are racist and can overreach, but they are in favor of the fair application of law enforcement.

A ballot initiative in Minneapolis, where George Floyd was murdered, sought to abolish the police department and replace it with a new Department of Public Safety, which would take a "comprehensive public health approach . . . including licensed peace officers if necessary." Voters roundly rejected the idea. Similarly, New York City elected Eric Adams, a

Black former NYPD captain who has no truck with "Defund," as its new crime-busting mayor.

Convinced of their rightness, "Defund" activists harmed their own side. The slogan "defund the police" has become a millstone swinging around the Democrats' neck, alienating those very same suburban swing voters who had turned against Donald Trump. Amid steep rises in crime during the coronavirus pandemic, Republicans weaponized the slogan as a campaign issue. The voting public largely agrees with them.

A study by the Democratic Congressional Campaign Committee, leaked to *Politico*, found that Republicans' culture war attacks on slogans such as "defund the police" were "alarmingly potent." It recommended Democratic candidates reaffirm their support of police officers.

Democrats are now recognizing "defund the police" for the threat it is. Rep. Richie Torres, the gay Black Latino congressman for the South Bronx, a self-proclaimed Progressive and champion for the urban poor, told MSNBC, "The defund police movement is dead in New York City — and good riddance." House Speaker Nancy Pelosi declared that — despite resistance from some Progressives like Missouri Rep. Cori Bush — "defund the police" was *not* the policy of the Democratic Party. President Biden not only traveled to New York to show support for Mayor Adams. Shortly afterward, he proclaimed in his State of the Union address: "The answer is not to defund the police. It's to fund the police. Fund them. Fund them."

James Clyburn, the veteran Black congressman to whom Biden owes his election as president, has warned that "defund the police" — despite being well meaning — poses a mortal threat to the racial-justice movement. He compared the term to the "burn, baby, burn" slogan that followed the Watts Riots against police brutality in Los Angeles in 1965. "'Burn baby burn' destroyed the student movement back in the 1960s," Clyburn tweeted. "If we're not careful, 'defund the police' could do the same thing here. We have a great movement that we should get behind. Let's not run the risk of losing it."

PART SIX

COUNT YOUR VICTORIES

There are very many ways to win. Don't needlessly disappoint yourself.

■

"DOUG SCHOEN FOR CONGRESS"

The New York Times *reported on my 1983 campaign for Congress, but endorsed one of my opponents—who also lost.*

Truth 43

LOSE THE BATTLE, WIN THE WAR

It is unrealistic in life to win every battle. What is important is to be able to turn any loss into an eventual win. Even tactical losses can contribute to strategic victory.

EVER SINCE CHILDHOOD, I had wanted to be a congressman. At family gatherings, I had watched my uncle Jack Bronston, a New York State senator, excuse himself from the dinner table to take important calls. His power to affect other people's lives seemed alluring to me.

Even as I set up a successful political consulting business and graduated from Harvard Law School, I was plotting a run for Congress. I calculated I could achieve that coveted power better as an elected official than as a political adviser behind the scenes. That was true then—but it is no longer necessarily true today.

At the age of twenty-six, I moved straight from Harvard to an apartment in the unfashionable Forest Hills neighborhood of Queens. My only reason was that I had identified the local Democratic congressman, Joseph P. Addabbo, as a vulnerable target. With the backing of the large Jewish community in Forest Hills, I figured I could topple him. The 1980 election, just a year after I moved into the area, was too soon. So I set my sights on the midterms of 1982.

Addabbo visited my new apartment in the smart neo-Gothic Forest Hills Inn on Seventy-First Avenue. I was hosting a meeting of a fringe Democrat reform group. I had paid $100,000 for the address—a hefty sum at the time for a pad in the outer boroughs of New York. I could see Addabbo prowling around my place thinking, "This guy is serious."

Addabbo managed to protect himself, however, with some basic gerrymandering. Before the 1982 midterms, his district was redrawn to exclude the largely Jewish Forest Hills and include more of the Italian Americans and African Americans who were his base. I now found myself in Forest Hills living in a district represented by nine-term incumbent and "machine Democrat" Ben Rosenthal. He was not an easy target. In late 1982, however, I became aware that Rosenthal was suffering from terminal cancer. That set up the prospect of a special election on his death. I held fire till then.

Rosenthal did indeed win a tenth term in 1982, but died just a day after the House of Representatives reconvened in 1983. My one and only race for Congress was finally on.

The official Democratic candidate in the special election was all but guaranteed to win. But the Democratic nomination was chosen in a backroom deal by the county committee, and particularly by its chairman, Donald Manes, the Queens Borough president. The Democratic front-runner, Alan

Havesi, decided not to run. So I went to kiss the ring to ask Manes for the Democratic nomination.

"As soon as I walked out of his office in Queens Borough Hall, I realized he had been soliciting a bribe."

At his office in Queens Borough Hall, Manes seemed perversely focused on how much I was worth, how much money my lawyer-father had, how much my uncle earned, and the private finances of a prominent land-use lawyer who worked with my father. He insisted on telling me how little he was paid as Borough president and boasted that he had a party-funded BMW and an unaudited American Express card on which he spent up to $100,000 a year.

Manes was encouraging—he even asked if I was interested in dating his daughter. But as soon as I walked out of his office in Queens Borough Hall, I realized he had been soliciting a bribe. His campaign aide Michael Nussbaum later invited me to a "walk-talk" to discuss possible arrangements further. I suppose if I had paid up I might have become a congressman and even Manes's son-in-law—but I declined the invitation.

So I found myself running against the official Democratic candidate, Gary Ackerman, a former junior high school teacher who had founded the local *Queens Tribune* newspaper and was then serving as a state senator. I set up the Queens Independent Party as a vehicle for myself, fundraised about $100,000 from friends, and spent a cool quarter of a million dollars of my own money to buy TV ads and put up posters. My theory was that, if I could get the endorsement of the Liberal Party, I had a chance of cobbling together enough votes as an Independent to beat the Democrat.

It was a theory I never got to test. Ray Harding, the head of the Liberal Party, was a friend and had agreed to endorse me. But he rapidly de-endorsed me and gave the Liberal line to Ackerman when incoming New York governor Mario Cuomo objected that I had worked for his rival Ed Koch. Meanwhile, the *New York Times* gave its endorsement to another outsider candidate, City Councilman Sheldon Leffler. Three weeks before the special election, taking on the Democratic machine in a Democratic seat, I recognized I had no chance.

It was a gut-wrenching experience running as a candidate for Congress. I had run campaigns for other people and imagined it would be easy. But I was too emotionally engaged and spending a lot of my own money. Every day when I drove past a giant "Vote for Ackerman" sign that my rival had hung across Queens Boulevard, I got upset. Nevertheless, when I lost the Liberal endorsement, I decided to persist.

It was important for me to fight this battle even though I knew I was going to lose. I had harbored the ambition to run for Congress since my teenage years. I knew I needed to see it through—to get it out of my system.

Ackerman won easily with 18,380 votes, or 50 percent. I came in third with 5,983, or 16 percent. I remember going to sleep that night saying to myself: "You know what? You took your shot. Now your whole future is ahead of you." Enriched by the experience of being a candidate myself, I was able to pivot to building my career as a political consultant. I turned my loss into a long-term victory. Just a decade after I lost my bid for Congress, I was working for President Clinton in the White House.

Six months after Ackerman's win, he called me to assure me I had a bright future ahead of me and invited me to serve on his finance committee—which I declined. Ten years later, I ran into Ackerman again while I was working in the Clinton White House. "Things have worked out really well for you," he observed. Twenty years after my election defeat, I met Ackerman again at an event. By then I had an international reputation. "Things have worked out *really* well for you," he said. "I'm envious." Thirty years after my loss, Ackerman, then leaving Congress, came to me again. This time, he asked me to help find him a job.

Almost all the other players in this skirmish in my life did not fare well. Manes killed himself with an eight-inch kitchen knife in the chest when he came under investigation for corruption. Havesi, who became New York City comptroller, was jailed in a "pay-to-play" scandal. Manes's aide Nussbaum was also convicted of soliciting a bribe. Liberal leader Harding pleaded guilty to helping facilitate illegal payments for Havesi but cooperated with prosecutors and avoided prison time. Two decades later, Leffler, who came in fourth in 1983 despite the *New York Times* endorsement, was sentenced to 540 hours of community service for campaign fraud in another race.

Ackerman, who beat me, went on to serve fifteen terms in the House of Representatives. He even got a street named after him in Central Islip, New York. In 2019, he was accused in a sex-abuse lawsuit of trying to force a seventeen-year-old boy to perform oral sex on him and then performing oral sex on the boy himself when he was a twenty-three-year-old Boy Scout leader. He denied the allegations.

Considering their fates, I obviously came out well ahead. I might have lost the battle, but I won the war.

CHARLES EVERS

Charles Evers, who replaced his assassinated brother, Medgar, as the field director of the Mississippi NAACP, and later ran for Mississippi governor, with his allies Dr. Martin Luther King and Senator Edward Kennedy at the Southern Christian Leadership Conference.

Truth 44

GET YOUR SHARE OF THE PIE

It is a popular saying in football that "Winning isn't everything. It's the only thing." That is cute, but not true. Winning may be everything, but it's certainly *not* the only thing. Often what we really want is not a winner-takes-all victory. We simply want what my old teacher Martin Kilson, the first Black professor to get tenure at Harvard, called "your fair piece of the pie."

THE FACT THAT Charles Evers had no chance of winning his 1971 race to become governor of Mississippi became obvious to me when I arrived as a wet-behind-the-ears eighteen-year-old who had never been south of the Mason-Dixon line before and was immediately appointed the campaign's research director.

Winning the election was not Evers's point.

Like many other young white civil rights activists before me, I had traveled to the Deep South to help Evers's struggle for Black empowerment. As a child, my mother had sat me in front of the television to educate me about the civil rights struggle. I still remember as a ten-year-old watching news reports of the assassination by a white racist of Evers's kid brother, civil rights leader Medgar Evers.

I had recently graduated from New York's tony Horace Mann prep school and was a freshman at Harvard—and I really had no idea where I was. I shared a room in a group house for Black kids with special needs run by a local reverend in Jackson. When I went out on a Sunday with my wad of newspapers, people would stare at this white boy who seemed so out of place. Many just assumed I was the paperboy. The experience was an eye-opener to me.

Evers, as we saw in our earlier chapter "Use Your Anger," was an imperious figure who had been an undertaker, a soldier in World War II, a bootlegger, a pimp, a nightclub owner, and a numbers runner for the Mob before becoming Mississippi's first Black mayor since Reconstruction. He was skeptical of the young, highly educated white liberals who came to help his campaign. His campaign seemed chaotic and there were tensions between the local Black activists and the whites who had come to help. But it was a new model in the politics of the Deep South: whites working for Blacks. Evers made it crystal clear to us: "You are not going to tell us that you know better than us—because you don't, by definition."

Evers had taken up the fight for civil rights in Mississippi when his brother was shot down. After two years as mayor of the small town of Fayette, he set his sights on the governorship. Evers ran as an independent. Black activists had been battling the state Democratic Party since the early 1960s, when Blacks were shut out of voting in the Democratic primaries that effectively chose the leaders of the Democrat-dominated state. Evers had helped form the rival, racially integrated Mississippi Freedom Democratic Party. In 1963, the MFDP set up its own polling stations in Black churches and schools and held a mock election for governor. At a time when Blacks could not register to vote officially, some 80,000 people voted. The following year, Evers's fellow-activist Fannie Lou Hamer, the twentieth child of a sharecropper, led an all-Black MFDP delegation to the Democratic National Convention in Atlantic City to challenge the state party's all-white delegation. President Lyndon Baines Johnson tried to broker a deal giving the MFDP two observer delegates—but the MFDP delegation walked. By running for governor himself in 1971, Evers was pushing something much bigger. He wanted to challenge Mississippi's entire white power structure.

His opponent in the governor's race was none other than the white Democrat Bill Waller—the district attorney who had twice unsuccessfully prosecuted the man who assassinated Evers's brother Medgar. Although white juries had deadlocked twice in the case, Charles Evers thought Waller was a decent man. It was to take decades, until 1991, and the revelation that the jury had been rigged, to convict Waller's original target, Byron De La Beckwith, of Medgar's murder.

Evers knew he stood no chance of becoming governor. When Waller won the Democratic primary, it was clear he had already lost the election. But Evers was not deterred. "Hell, no! We've already won," he told supporters. "Bill Waller likes Blacks. We already know that Mississippi's next governor will be the first one ever to like and respect us."

"He was able to show everyone in that neglected town that the notoriously racist police were duty-bound to protect a Black man."

As expected, Evers lost the election in a landslide, 77 to 22 percent. But Evers felt he had won just by running. Going toe-to-toe with a white Democrat had put them on an equal footing. I remember traveling to one night rally at a Black church in rural Copiah Country with a phalanx of white police officers escorting our motorcade through the darkness. For Evers, this was itself a victory: He was able to show everyone in that neglected town that the notoriously racist police were duty-bound to protect a Black man.

Despite his defeat, Evers believed he had taken another big step toward Black freedom and opened the way for the next Black person to run for and win the governorship. Riding Evers's coattails, some 300 other Blacks ran for public office in Mississippi on election day, from coroner and constable to tax assessor and circuit clerk. And about fifty of them actually won. Waller brought Blacks into his new administration and named three Blacks to the Mississippi Highway Patrol. In personal terms, it was a fulfillment of the promise Charles and Medgar Evers had made to each other as children: to fight to get their share. It taught me the enduring lesson that there is more to winning than victory.

BERNIE SANDERS

US Senator 2007–, US Representative 1991–2007

Bernie Sanders, six months after becoming the Socialist mayor of Burlington, Vermont, complained: "It hasn't been easy." He got a ticket on his car when he parked in the mayor's spot because a police officer could not believe the city's top elected official would have such an old jalopy.

Truth 45

WIN A LOT BY WINNING A LITTLE AT A TIME

We live in a short-term-ist culture, fixated on quarterly
results. But success is rarely instant, like winning the
Lotto. It is generally earned. Bernie Sanders's arch-foe in
the Senate, Mitch McConnell, calls it, in the title of his
autobiography, *The Long Game*.

THE BEGINNING of Bernie Sanders's political career was almost comic.

Sanders, a former student radical with curly hair and thick-framed glasses and a heavy Brooklyn accent, was invited by a friend to a political meeting of a Leftist anti-war group called the Liberty Union Party at Goddard College in Vermont. Sanders, just turned thirty, attended with his infant son, Levi, on his lap. Eager as always to share his views, Sanders raised his hand to speak to the roomful of strangers. An hour later, to his complete surprise, he had been nominated by a show of hands to be the party's candidate for the US Senate. He won "unanimously," he likes to say, because no one else wanted to go to all that trouble just to suffer an inevitable defeat.

Sanders's progress from a street-corner crank to arguably the most influential single member of the US Congress is seldom appreciated by pundits or the general public. With a series of small wins over decades, he has dragged the entire governing party to the Left and now arguably has more power in setting the agenda for the United States than the president himself. Even President Biden, who won election as a moderate, has, since taking office, begun to "feel the Bern."

The son of a Polish-Jewish paint salesman from Brooklyn, Sanders was certainly an unlikely candidate for Senate in largely rural Vermont in 1972. Republicans had held both Vermont's Senate seats for more than a century. Sanders, who had become an anti-war activist and civil rights campaigner at the University of Chicago, had bought an eighty-five-acre parcel of backcountry Vermont after living for several months on a kibbutz in Israel. One friend described him as a "back-to-the-lander." On his first-ever radio appearance, a caller to the talk show asked: "Who is this guy?"

Sanders earned just 2 percent of the vote in that first 1972 Senate race. Later that same year, Sanders ran as the Liberty Union candidate for governor—and got just 1 percent. However, Sanders insists his candidacy pushed the Democrats to embrace more popular left-wing policies, such as property tax reform and dental care for low-income children, which propelled the Democratic candidate to an upset victory. His gadfly role was a sign of things to come.

Always a politician who is happy to beat his head against the wall for a good cause, Sanders describes his early campaigns as "educational," rather than being designed to win. His fundamental message from the start has been: "The rich are getting richer and the poor are getting poorer."

He ran for Senate again in 1974, doubling his previous personal best to get 4 percent of the vote. In 1976, he ran again as the Liberty Union candidate for governor and set a new personal record of 6 percent. It was still a long, long way from victory. The Liberty Union was no longer attracting new members. He quit the party and left politics to devote himself to building a small business making educational filmstrips for schools, called the American People's Historical Society. When he discovered that few students had ever heard of his personal hero, Sanders made a half-hour video about Eugene Debs, founder of the American Socialist Party—and himself a five-time candidate for president of the United States in 1900, 1904, 1908, 1912, and 1920 (the last time, from jail).

"His fundamental message from the start has been: 'The rich are getting richer and the poor are getting poorer.'"

Ever the activist, Sanders reentered politics to run for mayor of Burlington in 1981. The presence of a second independent candidate split the vote and Sanders edged out the Democratic incumbent by twenty-two votes—which fell to just ten votes on the recount. The final result was 4,330 to 4,320.

In the year Ronald Reagan entered the White House, Sanders became a kind of anti-celebrity as America's only Socialist mayor. Garry Trudeau, in his syndicated *Doonesbury* comic strip, dubbed the city "The People's Republic of Burlington." "Yeah, okay, I'm a Socialist," Sanders told the *Boston Globe*. "We'll charge $10 a head to come see the freak mayor of Burlington." A police officer gave his rusty Volkswagen Dasher a ticket in the mayor's parking space at City Hall because he could not believe the jalopy could be the mayor's car.

As the mayor of Vermont's largest city, Sanders was well placed to win the state's only House seat, as he did in 1990, and go on to become one of its two senators, as he did in 2007. He was the only Socialist in Congress, and hung a photo of Eugene Debs in his office. In 2016, he became the first Socialist to win an Electoral College vote in US history when a "faithless elector" wrote in his name. His 2016 presidential campaign would quite likely have secured the Democratic Party nomination if the party rules had not been changed to Hillary Clinton's advantage. And, in this alternate universe, he might well have been president and the party's candidate in 2020 as well.

Despite his belief in a political revolution, Sanders has always achieved his goals incrementally. As a "movement politician," he focuses on coalition-building, changing the political culture, and mainstreaming his ideas. Once in Congress, he co-founded the Progressive Caucus. More recently, has formed an alliance with "The Squad" of Democratic Socialist congress-women, including Alexandria Ocasio-Cortez, who volunteered on his 2016 presidential campaign before being elected to Congress herself.

Sanders's tenacious but gradualist approach has yielded incredible success. His 2020 presidential race pushed other Democratic candidates to embrace "Medicare for All," free tuition, and the "Green New Deal." His opening position is always so extreme that even if he gets half a loaf, he has won. Until relatively recently, he was not even a member of the Democratic Party. Yet he has now achieved, if not complete ascendancy, a position of overwhelming strength in the Democratic Party. Like the real revolutionaries he has visited in Nicaragua and Cuba, he follows the old Socialist slogan, *la lucha continúa.*

"The struggle continues." Those were the very words Sanders used when he won election as Burlington mayor. And they were the very same words he used when he finally conceded the 2016 Democratic primary race to Hillary Clinton. They serve as the credo of Bernie's style of head-banging, stunningly successful, revolutionary incrementalism.

JON CORZINE

Governor of New Jersey 2006–2010, US Senator 2001–2006

Jon Corzine originally told me there was only a 5 percent chance he would run for the US Senate—but he announced his candidacy outside his home in Summit, New Jersey on September 23, 1999, and won.

Truth 46

UPSIDE SURPRISE YOURSELF

The most important benchmark of success is your own.
Don't allow others to define success for you. If you can
beat your own expectations, however you do that, you can
count yourself ahead.

THE FIRST TIME we ever spoke, Jon Corzine told me: "I'm about one in twenty in terms of doing this."

Corzine was being squeezed out as Chairman and CEO of the Wall Street investment bank Goldman, Sachs & Company and was looking around for something to do.

Powerful Democrats in New Jersey were trying to prevent a comeback by discredited former governor Jim Florio in the upcoming 2000 Senate race and were looking for an alternative candidate.

The matchmaking was done by Democratic fundraiser Orin Kramer, a former domestic policy adviser to President Jimmy Carter and a ubiquitous political power broker who prefers to keep his name out of the papers.

I was brought into the equation at a March 1999 fundraiser by New Jersey's hard-charging junior Democratic senator, Bob "The Torch" Torricelli, chairman of the Democratic Senatorial Campaign Committee, which was headlined by President Bill Clinton. Kramer turned to me and said innocently, "What about Jon Corzine?"

That is how candidates are often recruited. A whisper at a gathering of the party faithful. I was immediately intrigued.

Not only was Corzine a former protégé at Goldman Sachs of Clinton's treasury secretary, Bob Rubin, and a major Clinton donor, he was a self-made man who was brought up on the family farm in a small town in Illinois with more cows than people and had enlisted in the US Marine Corps Reserve. What is more, he had amassed a $400 million fortune on Wall Street that would enable him to finance his own campaign.

In politics, you need a horse to ride. Corzine seemed like a pedigree racehorse.

After several phone calls, we agreed to meet for breakfast at 6:45 sharp at the five-star Carlyle Hotel on New York's Upper East Side. We were too early even for the Carlyle, so we repaired to the much more downmarket Three Guys coffee shop nearby. Rather than the slick Wall Streeter I had expected, I found a man who was very sincere and immensely affable—but extremely tentative about the whole enterprise. I explained that he needed a benchmark poll to understand his position. A few days later, at a meeting in a poky office that Goldman Sachs appeared to reserve for cashiered executives, he asked me how much it would cost. I estimated $60,000 to $70,000. With no more ado, he pulled out a check, wrote out the amount, and handed it to me. "Good luck," he said. "Bring me the results."

The results of that first benchmark poll were not encouraging. New Jerseyans, and particularly New Jersey Democrats, were skeptical of being represented by a Wall Street investment banker. Running on a centrist platform, we found Corzine would lose the Democratic primary to the free-spending Florio by at least 25 percentage points. My recommendation, delivered at a meeting at New York's private members Harmonie Club, was that Corzine not enter the race.

Corzine, however, had other ideas. "Go back to the drawing board," he ordered.

I asked if he would authorize me to conduct another poll positioning him, despite his Wall Street background, as an out-and-out liberal. Since he had no record in public service to run on, this was not as difficult a stretch as it may seem. I enlisted Bob Shrum, the liberal *wunderkind* known for running populist big-issue campaigns who had drafted Senator Ted Kennedy's "The Dream Shall Never Die" speech for the 1980 Democratic convention. Corzine agreed to try out an unabashedly liberal message.

In our second benchmark poll, we tested a Corzine candidacy on a platform of universal health insurance, universal long-term care, universal college education, and universal gun control. We dubbed the policy "Universal Everything." When we added in some flattering details of biography, portraying him as an outsider passionate to bring change, he trailed primary rival Florio by just 3 percentage points.

"He sincerely embraced his new liberal persona. It was like he had found a new religion: 'CEO as Socialist.'"

A combination of Corzine's spending on TV ads, his homely personality that won over county Democratic leaders, and his program of "Universal Everything" saw him overturn what was once a 14–62 percent deficit to beat Florio to the Democratic nomination by 58–42 percent.

Normally, the winning primary candidate would tack back to the center for the general election to win over "swing voters." But we had taken Corzine so far to the left that it was impossible to credibly walk him back to the middle. He didn't mind at all. He sincerely embraced his new liberal persona. It was like he had found a new religion: "CEO as Socialist."

His opponent in the general election was Republican Bobby Franks, a popular, shrewd, and moderate local congressman. He ran on the clever slogan, "The best senator money can't buy." But Corzine blitzed him with grainy black-and-white TV ads linking him to Speaker of the House Newt Gingrich, the most unpopular Republican in America.

On election day, Corzine the Unabashed Liberal squeaked to victory by 50–47 percent—a massive underperformance in a state Democratic presidential candidate Al Gore won by 16 points. Corzine pulled off what had once seemed impossible. He became one of only a handful of self-financed Senate candidates who actually managed to win. Yet I remember on election night, his reaction was less one of jubilation than of relief. The onetime Wall Street trader—who had continually raised the stakes by spending a total of $36.7 million on this single Senate race—had won his long-odds bet.

JON CORZINE

Governor of New Jersey is one of the worst jobs in politics — but Jon Corzine went for it anyway, against my advice.

Truth 47

TO HAVE
IS TO HOLD

History is an endless catalog of leaders who have overreached. Innumerable are those who believe they can always get more. But once you conquer territory, your first obligation is to hold it—not jeopardize it to conquer more. Maintaining the ground you have already won counts as an important victory in itself.

IT IS VERY HARD to be unpopular as a US senator. You just need to turn up, shake hands, and see the folks at home regularly. You get to dole out ample portions of pork. If you are a Democrat in a Democratic state like New Jersey, once you have been elected senator you will be re-elected indefinitely.

Jon Corzine found himself in that happy position after our election win in 2000, as we saw in the previous chapter. But like many winners, he convinced himself that he would be a winner at everything always. So he did what leaders too often do: He overreached.

In 2005, while still sitting in the Senate, he ran for governor of New Jersey. I counseled against it.

He would win—but it was a victory that would effectively kill his political career.

In the previous chapter, we saw how Corzine won when he thought he might lose. In this chapter, we see how he lost when he was sure he had won.

The problem was that Corzine had convinced himself that he needed to become a governor if he was ever to run for president. No US senator had been elected president since John F. Kennedy in 1960, whereas Georgia governor Jimmy Carter, California governor Ronald Reagan, Arkansas governor Bill Clinton, and Texas governor George W. Bush had all more recently made it to the White House. Of course, Corzine called it wrong—the 2008 winner was first-term senator Barack Obama.

What Corzine's presidential ambition blinded him to was the fact that the New Jersey governorship is one of the worst jobs in elected politics, as toxic as the state's thousands of post-industrial brownfield sites. The last New Jersey governor to win the presidency was Woodrow Wilson in 1912.

I did some tracking polls for Corzine in his 2005 gubernatorial campaign. But by the time he hired me, it was too late to convince him that running for governor was a career blunder. When he won, he became responsible for New Jersey's $100 billion in debt and unfinanced pension and healthcare commitments. By the time he took office, the notoriously dysfunctional state was effectively bankrupt. He hiked sales tax by 1 percent and was unable to arrest the inexorable rise of local property taxes, the bane of every homeowner in the New Jersey suburbs. He alienated motorists by raising tolls on the state's iconic highways. With New Jersey's perennial budget woes compounded by the 2008 Global Financial Crisis, Corzine failed to win re-election the following year, losing to Republican Chris Christie.

"The New Jersey governorship is one of the worst jobs in elected politics, as toxic as the state's thousands of post-industrial brownfield sites."

If Corzine had just stayed in the Senate, he would surely have made it into the cabinet or onto the Democratic ticket as a vice presidential running mate. He may even have been able to run for president himself. I believe he would have served with distinction as treasury secretary, like his former Goldman Sachs mentor Bob Rubin. But he failed to hold on to what he had and his overreach led to the untimely demise of his political career.

SHIMON PERES

Israeli president and prime minister Shimon Peres worked for a peaceful "New Middle East" his whole life, but the Abraham Accords between Israel and Arab states were only concluded after his death. Here, Israeli national security adviser Meir Ben-Shabbat elbow bumps an Emirati official on a visit to Abu Dhabi, United Arab Emirates on September 1, 2020.

Truth 48

EVEN MOSES DIDN'T REACH THE PROMISED LAND

There is an old Wall Street saying: "Never wrong, just early."

Many times, victory will come too late for the victor to enjoy it. But it should be counted as victory nonetheless.

AT THE LABOR PARTY conference in Israel in 1997, Shimon Peres made the fatal mistake for a politician of asking the delegates: "Am I a loser?" A chorus of cries came back from the hall: "Yes!"

Peres, one of Israel's founding fathers, had by that point served as transport minister, finance minister, defense minister, and foreign minister, both twice, and two spells as prime minister. He would go on to spend a record forty-eight years in the Israeli Parliament, serving in twelve cabinets, and finally become the president of the country. Yet he was dogged by his reputation as a perennial loser. He fought five elections as Labor leader but failed to win any outright, scoring four defeats and one tie. The members of the Labor Party committee who yelled back at him were outraged at his most recent defeat in the 1996 election against Bibi Netanyahu, which—as we saw in the chapter on "When Available, Take Certainty"—he had been expected to win easily but bungled.

Peres, however, a self-declared optimist, never saw himself as a loser.

In my experience working for him during that 1996 election campaign, Peres never really was a practical politician. His reputation was as an "indefatigable schemer," as his longtime party rival Yitzhak Rabin famously called him. Truly, he was not a very effective one. He was a leader not because of his practical political skills, but because of his vision and the inspiration he provided to people.

For him, life was a battle for ideas—and many of his most unpopular and unlikely ideas eventually prevailed—starting with the creation of the state of Israel itself. Even if, just like the Prophet Moses, who died in sight of Jerusalem, Peres never quite arrived at his Promised Land of an Israel at peace in a "New Middle East."

In his life, Peres had taken on any number of seemingly impossible tasks—from arming the fledgling national Army in the months before Israel's War of Independence and equipping the new national Air Force to planning an improbable hostage rescue at Entebbe airport and convincing France to help build the Dimona reactor giving Israel a nuclear deterrent. He had tirelessly sought to place Israel in a peaceful and cooperative economic relationship with its Arab neighbors. As defense minister, he withdrew troops from Lebanon. As foreign minister, he secretly brokered the Oslo Peace Accords with the Palestinians, which won him a Nobel Peace Prize.

Although his causes often eventually prevailed, politically he seldom succeeded. Despite leading his party into five elections, he got only fleeting turns in the top job. His first taste of being prime minister came in 1977 when he unofficially filled in for two months when Rabin was forced to step down in a scandal. The first time he formally got the top job was a two-year time-share with Yitzhak Shamir after effectively tying with Shamir's Likud in the 1984 election. The only other time Peres served as prime minister was for the seven months after Rabin's assassination before losing the 1996 election.

"I am like a hunter—when a hunter wants to catch a bird, he shoots a few meters in front of it. The bird advances to where you have fired."

His political failure, such as it was, stemmed not so much from him as from mega-trends. Growing up on a kibbutz, Peres came from the Socialist Zionism of Israel's founders. He was a protégé of Israel's first prime minister, David Ben-Gurion, sometimes referring to himself as a "Ben Gurionist." Over the decades, Israel, like most of the rest of the world, moved away from this collectivist vision toward a more individualistic, capitalist, and nationalist model, empowering right-wing politicians. Yet he refused to be discouraged. After losing the 1996 election, he set up the Peres Center for Peace to promote his vision. In 2007, he was picked by the Knesset as president of Israel, when the incumbent was jailed for rape.

"I implemented most of the ideas I believed in," Peres said toward the end of his long life. "It took time. It was hard, but they were implemented. Some of those ideas looked crazy at the time. It's hard for me to describe the skepticism and resistance they met, like the aircraft industries matter, or Entebbe, or the nuclear issue, France, technology, Oslo—I saw all these things, I believed in them, I fought for them, I paid a price, they always criticize me, they tried to impose on me other intentions and to lower my voice. I wasn't frightened."

"I am like a hunter—when a hunter wants to catch a bird, he shoots a few meters in front of it. The bird advances to where you have fired. My job as I understand it is to shoot in front of the target because if you fire at the target, you will miss it. My whole way of thinking is to look ahead."

Even Peres's concept of a "New Middle East" of peaceful economic interdependence with Arab states and Israel aligned to defend themselves from Iran is now also starting to take shape—implemented in part by the so-called Abraham Accords. The 2020 deal between Israel and the United Arab Emirates and Bahrain, later joined by Sudan and Morocco, was brokered by leaders on the opposite side of politics to Peres: his old nemesis Bibi Netanyahu and Donald Trump, whom I have no doubt he would have disdained. Yet his vision prevailed.

HEIDI KLUM

Model, Actor, Presenter, Producer

Multi-hyphenate model Heidi Klum waving the Sports Illustrated *cover that made her a superstar.*

Truth 49

THERE IS
NO WINNING
WITHOUT LOVE

Victory has as many dimensions as life itself. It is hard to

count yourself successful if you are loveless and friendless.

Prize your private life as much as your public success.

I INTERVIEWED Heidi Klum some years ago for my book on *What Makes You Tick?* The German supermodel, actress, multi-millionaire businesswoman, and Emmy-winning TV host issued an important corrective for many of the obsessive world leaders I frequent. "Having money and a successful career is no success," she insisted, "if you don't have love around you."

Klum has literally been winning since her teenage years. She was raised in an arts-and-craftsy household in a small town outside Cologne, the daughter of a hairdresser and a cosmetics executive. She used to make her own clothes for her Barbie doll. As a girl of seventeen, she noticed a coupon in a magazine for a TV modeling contest and cut it out. For a lark, she climbed into her bathing suit and dancing stockings and hitched up her then-chestnut hair and her girlfriend took pictures of her on the couch.

The "Model 92" contest was a much bigger deal than she realized. After driving five hours to Munich for the audition, she discovered the finalists would appear on the popular late-night show of Thomas Gottschalk—Germany's Jay Leno. It was sponsored by the German women's magazine *Petra.* There were 25,000 contestants. Klum won. Still noticeably shy and having just turned eighteen, she earned a $300,000 modeling contract.

The modeling agency already had tall, skinny superstars like Claudia Schiffer and Eva Herzigová who were much in demand for the runway shows. Klum had boobs and hips. "She is no runway model!" German designer Wolfgang Joop told the newspaper *Bild.* "Heidi Klum is simply too heavy and has too big a bust. And she always grins so stupidly. That is not avant-garde—that is commercial!" Fellow designer Karl Lagerfeld endorsed that view.

"As a girl of seventeen, she noticed a coupon in a magazine for a TV modeling contest and cut it out."

There was much more to Klum, however, than her nickname, "The Body." She steered herself toward advertising and magazine work. She went to more castings than other models and was more pushy. She told herself, "I might be pretty, but I can't be prettier than all the other girls out there."

She was, she told me, just "more inventive."

Her breakthrough came in 1998, a year after she started modeling for Victoria's Secret lingerie, when she adorned the cover of *Sports Illustrated's* Swimsuit Issue. Klum parlayed her fame into other businesses. She co-authored a book and launched several clothing lines, jewelry, and two fragrances. She played a bad-tempered hair model in the movie *Blow Dry* and made cameo appearances in Hollywood hits such as *The Devil Wears Prada*, *Ocean's Eight*, and TV shows *Desperate Housewives* and *Sex and the City*. She replaced Sharon Osbourne as a judge on *America's Got Talent* and won an Emmy as the host of the *Project Runway* Reality TV show.

In keeping with her philosophy, Klum, a mother of four, has always focused, however, on her personal happiness. When she was married to the British singer-songwriter Seal, she suggested they shoot a romantic music video for his hit "Secret" of them canoodling naked in bed so they could one day show their kids. The couple subsequently broke up and she dated her bodyguard for two years before marrying Tokio Hotel guitarist Tom Kaulitz in a ceremony aboard Aristotle Onassis's old super-yacht, the *Christina O.* She was forty-six; her new husband twenty-nine.

"STOP THE STEAL"

Jacob Chansley, aka Jake Angeli, dubbed the "QAnon Shaman," invaded Congress on January 6, 2021, to "stop the steal" and overturn the presidential election. He was sentenced to three-and-a-half years in jail.

Truth 50

THE OPPOSITE
IS ALSO TRUE

No one can be right all the time. Military planners war-game
their strategies with hostile "Red Teams" to discover where
they are weak. "Red Team" yourself. Recognizing when you
are wrong—and why—is itself a victory.

AS VICE PRESIDENT Mike Pence presided over a joint session of Congress to certify the 2020 election results, Jake Angeli joined the mob scaling the scaffolding outside. Wearing a Viking headdress with horns and fur, red, white, and blue warpaint, completely bare-chested, and carrying an American flag tied to a spear, he was among the first thirty protesters to break into the US Capitol. Within minutes, Pence was evacuated by armed police and the self-styled "QAnon Shaman" was sitting in the very chair where the vice president had been, screaming "Freedom!"

It was the first time the US Congress had been stormed since the British sacked the building in 1814.

The several thousand Trump loyalists who occupied the Congress on January 6, 2021, were convinced that Democrat Joe Biden had won by fraud. At the precise moment they were threatening the very foundation of America's democracy, they were sure they were acting to save it. Most had just attended Trump's own "Save America" rally at the Ellipse earlier in the day, where the outgoing president had exhorted them: "We fight like hell and if you don't fight like hell, you're not going to have a country anymore." As we saw in an earlier chapter, "People Only Do Bad When They Think They Are Doing Good."

"It was the first time the US Congress had been stormed since the British sacked the building in 1814."

It is, of course, absurd to suggest that Biden won the 2020 election by fraud or any other skulduggery. It is a proposition that has been thrown out of court dozens of times. A survey by *USA Today* counted sixty-two pro-Trump election lawsuits, of which sixty-one were thrown out. (The sole victory came in a Pennsylvania ruling that voters could not "cure" their ballots if they had failed to provide identification within three days of the election.) Even Mitch McConnell, the top Republican in the Senate, has repeatedly insisted that the riot was a violent insurrection aimed at stopping the peaceful transfer of power.

At first many Washington players thought Trump's campaign to "stop the steal" would just fade away when he left the White House. Instead, the Republican Party has rallied to this convenient fiction—even though Biden won the election by more than 7 million votes (and by 306 to 232 Electoral College votes). Republicans who reject the "stop the steal" claims, like Rep. Adam Kinzinger and Rep. Liz Cheney, are being forced out of Congress by the party. Both were censured by the Republican National Committee merely for taking part in the congressional January 6 committee. McConnell himself is also likely to be pushed out of his leadership position. Even Republicans like Ted Cruz, whose objection to the Arizona result was being debated when the Senate was assaulted, have cravenly backed away from calling the riot an attack (as we saw in the chapter "You Have to Give to Get"). The Republican National Committee passed a resolution calling the January 6 protest "legitimate political discourse."

Trump has shamelessly fueled this "Lost Cause" myth because it enables him to raise funds and stay relevant. It motivates his base by making them ever more alienated from the political system. Polling shows some two-thirds of Republicans believe the 2020 election was "stolen."

It is quite possible, in my view, that the Republicans can sustain their denial of the 2020 election result indefinitely. "Stop the steal" will remain a theme of Republican politics while it remains useful to Trump and the party, and then just fade out.

However, the law courts tell a story that is 180 degrees different—and could dramatically change the politics. So far, at least 725 members of the January 6 mob have been prosecuted for occupying Congress, with stiff sentences handed down. The FBI has appealed for the public's help in identifying hundreds more. Members of militia groups like the Proud Boys and the Oath-Keepers have been charged with the crime of sedition.

Even Trump himself faces possible legal jeopardy from the criminal investigation into his phone call telling the Georgia secretary of state, Brad Raffensperger, "I just want to find 11,780 votes." Lawyers for the House of Representatives' January 6 committee have said in a court filing that there is evidence for potential criminal charges against Trump for obstruction of an official proceeding and conspiracy to defraud the American people.

Jesse Angeli, the "QAnon Shaman," has already been dealt a hard lesson. He pleaded guilty to one charge of obstructing an official proceeding and is now serving three-and-a-half years in jail. Ironically, Angeli, whose birth name is Jacob Chansley, left a note on Pence's desk during the uprising. It read: "It's only a matter of time, justice is coming."

He just did not realize that justice was coming for *him*!

AFTERWORD

WE HAVE TRAVELED the world together in these chapters to learn the lessons of the leaders I have worked with, hopscotching the United States from far Right to extreme Left, and circling the globe from Mexico to South Africa to Israel to Serbia to Turkey to South Korea and back home again. Though some of the settings may seem exotic, the dynamics of power are the same worldwide.

Power can, from the outside, seem very mysterious and breed all kinds of conspiracy theories. In truth, it is not. Power is very predictable.

It is as stable as physics—and its natural laws as knowable. In the seemingly chaotic clash of interests, an understanding of the underlying dynamics of power enables you to maximize your chance of a successful outcome.

All of the fifty truths enunciated above should, in theory, apply to every one of these situations and each personality. I have obviously chosen what I think are the best examples to demonstrate either the wisdom of following these rules, or the folly of ignoring them.

"Power can, from the outside, seem very mysterious and breed all kinds of conspiracy theories. In truth, it is not. Power is very predictable."

It is true that you can get away with things in some political settings that would be impossible in others, such as blatantly stealing elections. For this reason, I have omitted my experiences working in Venezuela and Zimbabwe. But don't imagine that, in any country, including the United States, the impossible is always impossible.

If you have read this far you will have realized that we have learned as much from leaders' mistakes as from their achievements. Do the same with your own mistakes. It is frustrating for a political consultant who must bend to the will of his client, even if they are clearly wrong. But you are your own client: You get to decide for yourself.

We have also learned not just from the leaders I have advised but also from their opponents. Sometimes my clients made no obvious mistakes but their rivals simply outplayed them in the power game. Respect. You should learn from your enemies too.

Most of all, we have learned to account for human frailty, greed, and desperation, including, indeed especially, our own.

I have written about big-time politics because that has been my business for half a century. But the same power dynamics prevail in every sphere of human interaction. You can use these fifty principles in your work, your social life, your school.

Sometimes, it will not be immediately clear which truth is most applicable to a particular dilemma. Sometimes, different truths might argue for different courses of action, and a judgment call must be made. That is good, because the fundamental requirement to successfully navigate this world is always to think it through.

That is what I am paid to do.

ACKNOWLEDGMENTS

A special note of gratitude to the many people whose lives I write about. I often reflect on our experiences together with a combination of awe, respect, admiration, and, at times, incredulity.